Campus Planning in an Urban Area

prepared by
Doxiadis Associates, Inc.

The Praeger Special Studies program—utilizing the most modern and efficient book production techniques and a selective worldwide distribution network—makes available to the academic, government, and business communities significant, timely research in U.S. and international economic, social, and political development.

Campus Planning in an Urban Area

A Master Plan for Rensselaer Polytechnic Institute

Praeger Publishers New York Washington London

PRAEGER SPECIAL STUDIES IN U.S. ECONOMIC AND SOCIAL DEVELOPMENT

PRAEGER PUBLISHERS
111 Fourth Avenue, New York, N.Y. 10003, U.S.A.
5, Cromwell Place, London S.W.7, England

Published in the United States of America in 1971
by Praeger Publishers, Inc.

© 1971 by Praeger Publishers, Inc.

Library of Congress Catalog Card Number: 79-153391

Printed in Greece

Foreword

Long-range planning at a university is, at best, a nebulous endeavor; so much of the future is unknown, so much of the present is in unpredictable transition, and so much of the past is no longer relevant. Long-range planning in higher education can provide little more than guidelines to those who must make present decisions that have long-range implications.

Rensselaer Polytechnic Institute (R.P.I.), a technological university in Troy, New York, has long concentrated on the preparation of engineers, scientists, architects, and managers for professional careers dedicated to the application of technology and science to the service of man. It plans to continue to perform this needed social function for many years to come. This expectation is the principal guideline for its long-range planning.

The campus of an urban university expresses something about the quality of its academic life, as well as its role as a citizen of the community in which it is located. The campus also represents many different things to the various groups of people who live, learn, teach, or visit there. It plays the role of home, museum, place of employment, social center, library, sports center, park, arena for dissent, and forum for the search for truth. All of these functions must be accommodated on a campus designed not only for today but also for the future.

The campus master plan proposed by Doxiadis Associates in June, 1969, represented a cooperative effort based upon an initial set of long-range planning assumptions, guidelines, studies, projections, and conferences. These inputs were translated into a proposed long-range land-acquisition and -use concept for R.P.I. During the 1969-70 academic year, this proposed concept was subjected to intensive analysis and debate by the Board of Trustees, faculty, students, alumni, and staff.

The principal value of the proposal at that stage was that it gave the members of the R.P.I. community a visualization of the kind of ideal campus environment that could emerge from the concept. As an exercise in over-all analysis, the proposal enabled them to focus on the most significant factors affecting R.P.I.'s present and future land use. Their ideas, criticisms, and suggestions have given the planners a more realistic and generally accepted basis for translating R.P.I.'s needs and desires into a revised campus master-plan concept.

The R.P.I. campus master plan has already become a valuable point of reference in the University's decision-making and planning processes. This has been so despite the prospect of continuous revision, since a master plan, in order to continue to be of maximum value, must be able to reflect the dynamics of change in educational concepts and the physical environment, as well as the needs and desires of those who are concerned with them. The campus master plan proposed for R.P.I. by Doxiadis Associates and the process thus far developed for its revision represent important steps in the achievement of this objective.

Rogers B. Finch
Vice-President of Planning
Rensselaer Polytechnic Institute
Troy, New York

January, 1971

Preface

Rensselaer Polytechnic Institute is a coeducational university in the city of Troy, located in the Hudson River Valley in the northeastern part of the state of New York. In 1824, Stephen Van Rensselaer, a public-spirited landowner of the upper Hudson Valley and an influential citizen of the area, wrote: «I have established a school at the north end of Troy, in Rensselaer County in the building usually called the Old Bank Place for the purpose of instructing persons who may choose to apply themselves in the application of science to the common purposes of life.» Today, this school exists as Rensselaer Polytechnic Institute, a private, nonsectarian, coeducational institution, providing courses at undergraduate and graduate levels to about 4,500 students. In 1965, the title «Technological University» was officially attached to R.P.I. by a decision of the Board of Trustees. The campus is situated near the central business district of the city and is spread over several irregular lots. Its present enrollment, including the graduate school, numbers nearly 5,000 students.

The University, in its desire for an orderly expansion of its campus and physical plant facilities, tried to develop an up-to-date master plan and program. To achieve this, R.P.I. appointed Doxiadis Associates, Inc., of Washington, D.C., as consultants. Their assignment was the fulfillment of the physical expression of R.P.I.'s goals and the development of an academic campus in which grounds and facilities would be efficiently organized and in harmony with the city.

In brief, the primary task on hand was to develop a plan for land organization of the present University holdings, campus land uses and boundaries, a clear pedestrian and vehicular pattern of movement, locations and size of new buildings, and an implementation program for the above-described proposals. This study, therefore, provides in a single document the assumptions, guidelines, and logical sequence of thought culminating in the master plan for the development of the R.P.I. campus.

For consistency and clarity, the terms used most often in this document are defined or referred to as follows:

1. R.P.I. refers to Rensselaer Polytechnic Institute, Troy, New York.
2. University refers to R.P.I., which in 1965, by a decision of the Board of Trustees, attached to its name the title «Technological University.»
3. Consultants refer to Doxiadis Associates, Athens, Greece, and Doxiadis Associates, Inc., Washington, D.C.

Following this appointment, the consultants made several survey visits to R.P.I. during the first few months and collected relevant data. These surveys and interviews culminated in a work conference held at the campus in August, 1968, at which matters concerning the University's actual physical plant and its relationship to the city and the region were discussed.

On the principle that the University must participate in all phases of the development of the master plan, a second work conference was held in October, 1968. The subject on this occasion was the traffic problem of the University and, particularly, ways of connecting the campus with the nort-south arterial highway that passes close to the western boundary of R.P.I. property, as proposed by the state of New York. Another group of work conferences was also held in October, 1968, to discuss the development of the master plan and to establish future academic needs and priorities.

In November, 1968, a questionnaire was given to every student at R.P.I. asking him to note his daily movements within a cycle of one week. The data were processed at the Computer Center of the Doxiadis Associates headquarters in Athens. These data were eventually used for a mathematical model devised for evaluating the efficiency of alternate schematic site plans showing new building units on the campus. (See the Appendix at the end of this study.)

Conferences were held during February, 1969, on the subject of a land policy for R.P.I., where the consultants presented to the University administration two alternate layouts, in schematic form, for campus development, illustrating the methodology used for the evaluation of their efficiency with the aid of a mathematical model. Finally, in the following month, a summary of all the above steps was presented to the Committee on Physical Facilities. The comments made at all the above conferences, presentations, and informal discussions were incorporated in the proposal. This book, however, does not contain decisions or commitments on the part of R.P.I. Continuous collaboration over the past months between the consultants and the administration was only to provide a clearer understanding of the problem.

This volume contains the consultants' proposals as a whole, and, although it incorporates highlights of additional studies made for R.P.I., it is intended as an all-inclusive, self-sufficient document. In addition to this preface, the contents of the document are as follows: Chapter I contains an analysis of existing conditions that should be taken into consideration for planning purposes. R.P.I. is viewed within the region, the city of Troy, and the particular neighborhood of the city. The conditions prevailing within the property boundaries are analyzed in greater detail. Chapter 2 contains the assumptions drawn concerning long-range planning, a graduation from general to particular types of assumptions. Chapter 3 introduces future building requirements for R.P.I. These needs are expressed in the different kinds of areas that compose the campus's physical plant. Chapter 4 contains the highlights of the logical sequence of thought that led to the proposed master plan. Chapter 5 is a concluding statement about the proposal. Finally, the Appendix gives a detailed account of the development of a mathematical model as an aid to campus planning.

Acknowledgments

The project was carried out in Washington, D.C., and Athens, Greece, by the consultants' teams, under the personal direction of C. A. Doxiadis, President, and S. Chatiras, Senior Vice-President, of Doxiadis Associates. Andreas N. Simeon, then Executive Vice-President of Doxiadis Associates, Inc., also took an active part in all phases of the planning of this project. The project planner of the study and author of this document was C. B. Maniotes, architect-planner. The team that performed the relevant work, research, and so on, consisted of the following: P. Alexiou, architect; E. de Venguechea, architect-planner; J. Dokoumetzidis, traffic engineer; A. Drymiotis, system analyst; J. Frantzeskakis, traffic engineer; E. Glyniadakis, architect; and I. Tazartes, system analyst. A. Christakis and S. Wilks of Doxiadis System Development Corporation also offered their assistance for the collection of basic data and the elaboration of the mathematical model for the evaluation of the efficiency of the alternative campus layouts.

Significant contribution was made, in the early phases of the organization and planning of the study, by A. Demetriou, former Vice-President of Doxiadis Associates, Inc., Washington, D.C. Alfred W. Baxter, of Baxter, McDonald and Company, Berkeley, California, also assisted in the preliminary analysis of the utilization of academic facilities.

The consultants wish to express their wholehearted appreciation for the unfailing assistance granted them by R. G. Folsom, President of R.P.I. Deep appreciation is expressed for the cooperation given by C. H. Daniel, Vice-President and Business Manager of R.P.I., and R. B. Finch, Vice-President of Planning. The assistance given by various other officials of R.P.I., particularly Dennis P. Jones, Assistant Business Manager, and D. G. Ramroth, Director of Physical Plant, is also acknowledged.

Contents

LIST OF TABLES

LIST OF MAPS

Part I

THE PRESENT SITUATION

Chapter 1 Background and Conditions in the Area and on Campus

This chapter analyzes the background and conditions in the area and on the campus that influence the planning process. It examines the setting of the R.P.I. campus in the region, in the city of Troy, and in the particular neighborhood that it occupies within the city. Greater analytic detail is outlined for the conditions within the boundaries of the R.P.I. campus. In this area, in addition to the physical setting, matters of academic organization, composition of student body, and physical plant are examined closely.

TRI-CITY AREA

The area that includes the intersection of the Mohawk and Hudson rivers and the cities of Albany, Schenectady, and Troy is known as the Tri-City Area. (*See Map 1.*) Troy is located on the eastern bank of the Hudson River. About five miles south across the river lies Albany, the capital of the state of New York; Schenectady is located ten miles due west.

It is no accident that the Tri-City Area has come to function as a major transportation center for the northeastern United States; the presence of the two rivers and the area's morphological configuration have greatly influenced the direction and character of the transportation development. Major regional roads bring traffic to this area from Montreal, Boston, New York City, and a chain of large cities along an axis westward to Chicago.

The importance of this area is reflected also, to a large extent, by the role of Albany as a governmental and service center. A concentration of higher educational institutions is found in this general vicinity; within the Tri-City Area there is an association of cooperating higher educational units. The Hudson-Mohawk Association of Colleges and Universities is composed of Albany Law School, Albany Medical School, Albany Pharmacy School, College of Saint Rose, R.P.I., Russell Sage College, Saint Bernardine of Siena College, Skidmore College, and Union College. The association recognizes the distinctive and individual forms, responsibilities, and purposes of its members and tries to explore, develop, and implement cooperative activities and programs of a mutually beneficial nature in either academic or nonacademic fields of interest.

CITY OF TROY

The city of Troy is located on the eastern bank of the Hudson River, in the upper Hudson Valley. Its population declined from 72,300 to 67,500 in the period between the years 1950 and 1960. This is slightly above the total population decline experienced in the entire period between 1910 and 1950. One of the basic causes of the decline in the city's population is the weakening and contraction of its economic base resulting from the reduction of employment by industries in the area. Other factors that have also accelerated the population decline include problems of deterioration and an inadequate living environment, which have forced a substantial number of former residents to move to the suburbs.

The development of the city of Troy has largely been influenced by topographic features. The flat land along the river was the first area to be built up. Streets were laid out in a direction parallel to the river. As the city grew eastward, the new streets followed ridges and valleys toward the neighboring hills.

The land-use pattern also follows this trend of development. Industrial and railroad uses have formed along the riverfront. The commercial core of the city is also located close to the river, in an area where the river bank consists of a wide flat area permitting the development of a central business district. Residential areas begin at the eastern fringe of the downtown area and spread to the north and south along the flat lands.

This development is governed by a zoning ordinance. (*See Map 2.*) Basically, the zoning ordinance recognizes only three types of land uses — residential, business, and industrial — with subzones for each use. Several institutions within the city limits are ignored as entities, and the land in their possession is described as a residential zone requiring a variance to be granted by the city for building. This situation should be altered in the future by zoning the property of these institutions as land for institutional use.

A rigid gridiron pattern of streets was laid out on the flat bank of the river, which contains the central business district of the city of Troy. The steep hills that begin east of the downtown area prevented the continuation of this street pattern; as a result, an irregular network of streets evolved by following the contours of the ground.

The streets of the level land alongside the river are subject to extremely heavy traffic, particularly in a north-south direction. The east-west traffic near the central business district and the R.P.I. campus has to utilize two of the five Hudson River bridges and the few radial streets running east of the center.

Two of the most problematic street intersections in the city of Troy are in the vicinity of the R.P.I. campus. (*See Map 3.*) The intersection of Fifteenth and Congress streets is the most deficient, followed by that of Fifteenth Street and College Avenue, which is rated as one of the seven most hazardous intersections in the city of Troy. As early as 1960, when the street-capacity and traffic-volume survey was conducted by the New York State Department of Public Works, the capacity of Fifteenth Street was almost exhausted. The deficiency in the two bridges and the intersection of Congress and Fifteenth streets, among other areas, is shown in red on the map indicating street capacities and traffic volumes.

R.P.I.: COMPOSITION OF THE CAMPUS

The R.P.I. campus is situated in the heart of the city of Troy. To locate the University, one may say that the campus falls roughly in the area delimited by Eighth Street, College Avenue, Bouton Road, Tibbits Avenue, Peoples Avenue, and Hoosick Street. The actual property consists of many irregular plots, with a total area of approximately 245 acres.

The two parallel north-south streets, Fifteenth Street and Burdett Avenue, divide the already scattered property composing the present campus into three major parts: the first part, an area of seventy-four acres, lies between Eighth and Fifteenth streets; the second falls between Fifteenth Street and Burdett Avenue; and the third part, an area of 139 acres, lies between Burdett and Tibbits avenues.

The second part, the one between Fifteenth Street and Burdett Avenue, is not a unified plot of land; it is a conglomeration of lots, varying in size, whose total area covers approximately thirty-two acres. This part of the campus is the weak link between the two large plots of R.P.I. property. More than half of the area in this sector is non-University property.

Scattered among R.P.I. property are several plots of land owned by the University's «best relatives,» the student fraternities. The total area of this land is approximately eleven acres. The actual boundaries of R.P.I. property are not defined by landmarks or by easily recognizable limits. In some cases, the property lines coincide with fences; in others, it is only a line recorded in the deed of property.

The land-use pattern in the vicinity of the R.P.I. campus is primarily residential, with the exception of the area adjacent to the western boundary of the campus, which is the eastern edge of the central business district of Troy. This area is in need of urgent revitalization; the related problems of blight, congestion, and an inadequate living environment have become increasingly apparent in recent years. The city of Troy has already zoned three large tracts of land for reconstruction — Urban Renewal Projects A, B, and C. (*See Map 4.*)

Several institutional land uses surround the present R.P.I. property. To the south are Public School 14, the New York State Armory, and Troy High School, occupying 4, 10, and 42 acres of land, respectively. To the east is the Jewish Home for the Aged, occupying a plot of land approximately 15 acres. Across Peoples Avenue, to the north, is a 12-acre plot of land occupied by the Samaritan Hospital. Two parks are in the vicinity of the R.P.I. campus: Prospect Park toward the south, which includes public recreation areas such as playfields and tennis and basketball courts, and Beman Park toward the north, with trees, benches, walks, and so on, for those seeking more passive recreation.

The existing use of R.P.I. property has a set pattern of land utilization. These uses readily fall into five categories: academic, student housing, central facilities (including student and service functions), athletic and playfields, and faculty housing. (*See Map 5.*) The western part of the campus, particularly the area included between Eighth and Fifteenth streets and Sage and College avenues, is the academic area. The eastern part of the campus, the area included between Burdett and Tibbits avenues, may be characterized as follows: the northwestern part as athletic and playfields and the western part as student housing. On

MAP 1
Tri-City Area: Troy, Albany, Schenectady — showing Hudson-Mohawk Association of Colleges and Universities and Major Transportation Routes

Higher Educational Institutions	●
Albany Pharmacy School	1
Albany Law School	1
Albany Medical School	1
Russell Sage College	2
College of Saint Rose	3
Saint Bernardine of Siena College	4
Union College	5
R.P.I. Campus	
City Limits of Troy, New York	
Existing Limited-Access Highways	
Limited-Access Highways Under Construction	
Limited-Access Highways Proposed	
Other Main Highways	
Regional Airport	

N

DOXIADIS ASSOCIATES INC. — WASHINGTON DC.

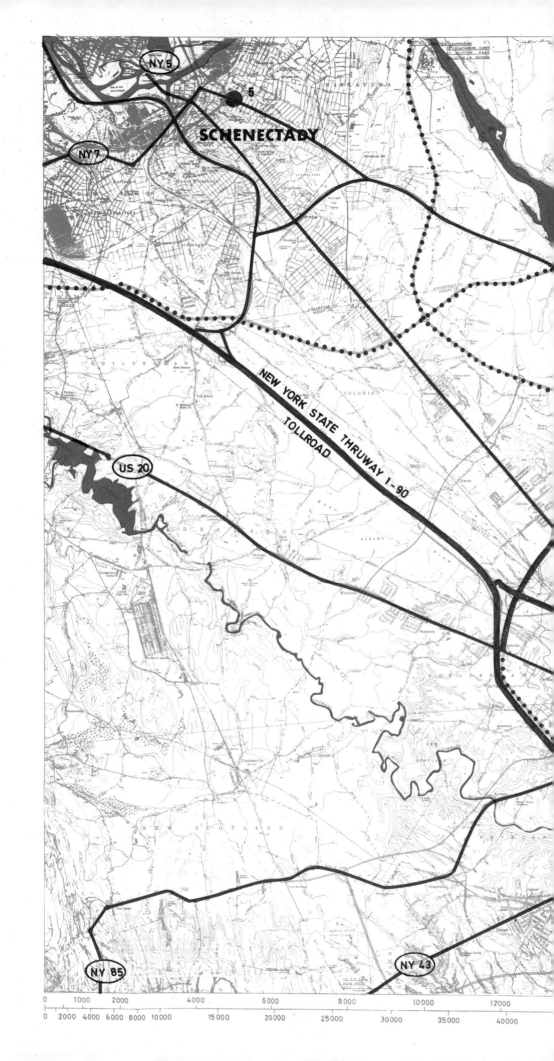

NY 5

5

SCHENECTADY

NY 7

NEW YORK STATE THRUWAY I - 90

US 20

NY 85

NY 43

0	1000	2000	4000	6000	8000	10000	12000

0	2000	4000	6000	8000	10000	15000	20000	25000	30000	35000	40000

MAP 2
City of Troy: Zoning Map, As Approved July, 1966

R.P.I. Campus

Residence Zone No. 1

Residence Zone No. 2

Residence Zone No. 3

Residence Zone No. 4

Residence Zone No. 5

Business Zone No. 1

Business Zone No. 2

Light Industrial Zone No. 1

Heavy Industrial Zone No. 2

Note: Number of zones refer to city zoning ordinance

N

0   1000   2000   3000   4000   Meters

0   1000 2000   4000   6000   8000   10000   12000   14000 Feet

DOXIADIS ASSOCIATES INC.— WASHINGTON DC.

MAP 3
**City of Troy: Street Capacity and
Traffic Volumes During Peak Hour**

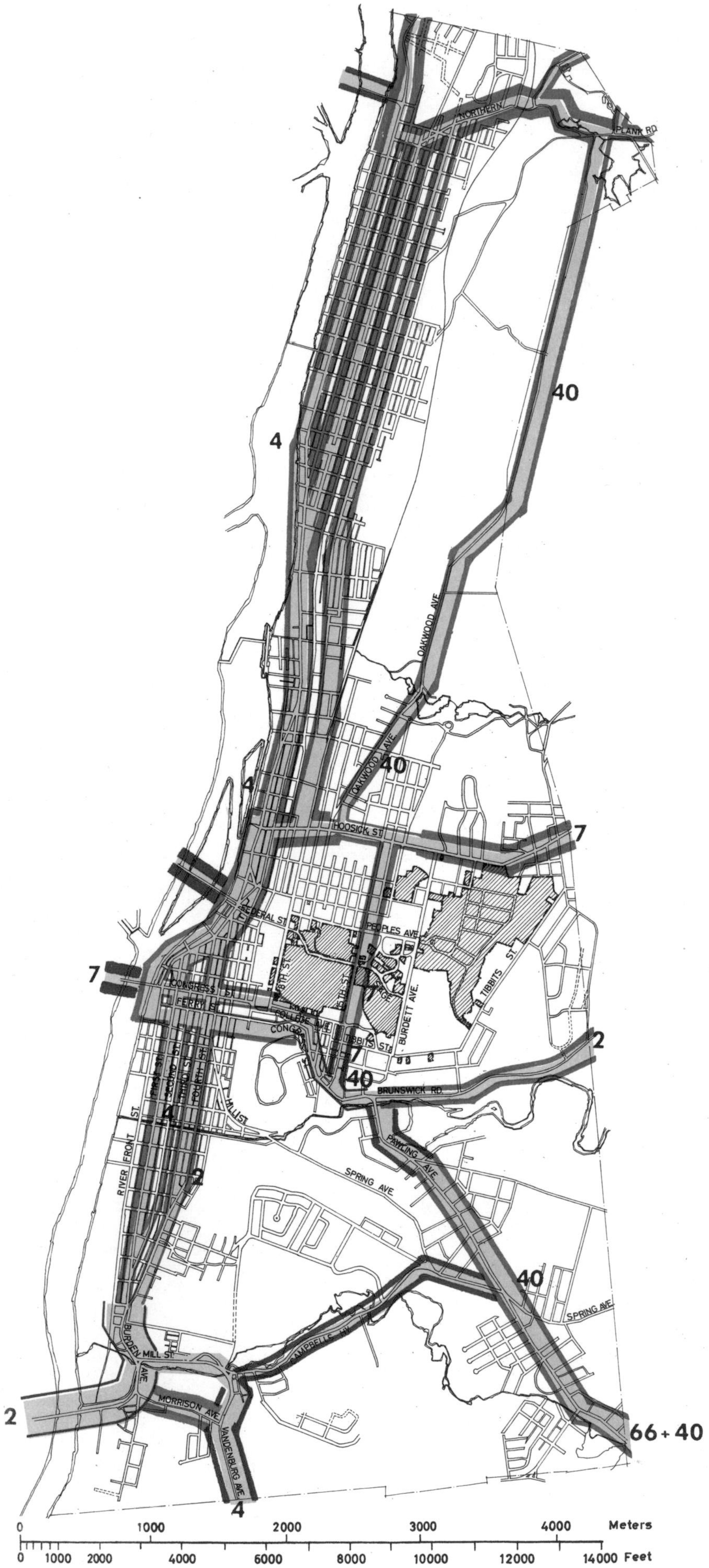

40

4

4

40

7

4

7

40

2

7

40

2

40

2

66 + 40

4

R.P.I. Campus

Vehicular Volumes
(In Hundreds/hr)   5   10   15

Deficiency in Street
Capacity   5   10   15

Reserve in Street
Capacity   5   10   15

Source : New York State
Department of Public Works

Note : Numbers identify major
highways

0   1000   2000   3000   4000   Meters

0   1000 2000   4000   6000   8000   10000   12000   14000 Feet

DOXIADIS ASSOCIATES INC.—WASHINGTON DC.

MAP 4
R.P.I. Campus: Existing Land Uses in Vicinity

University Property

Student Fraternity
Property

Religious, Related to
R.P.I.

Housing

Commercial

Industrial

Institutional, Education,
Health, Religious

Parks, Cemeteries

Urban-Renewal Projects:
A,B,C.

N

3000

9500   10 000

DOXIADIS ASSOCIATES INC.-WASHINGTON DC.

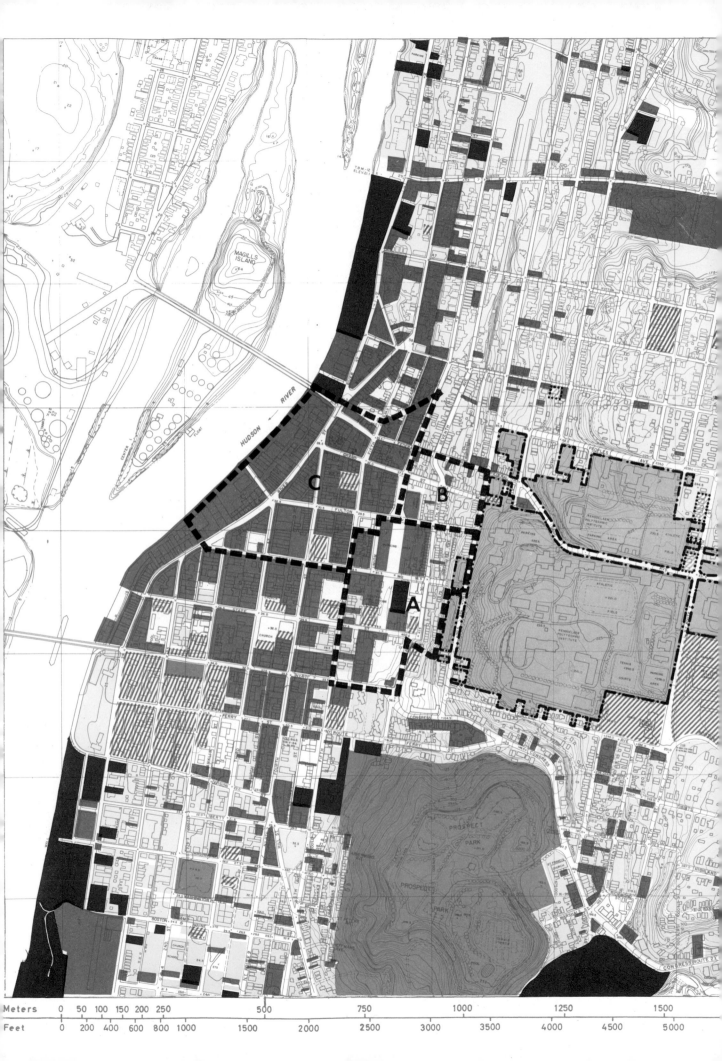

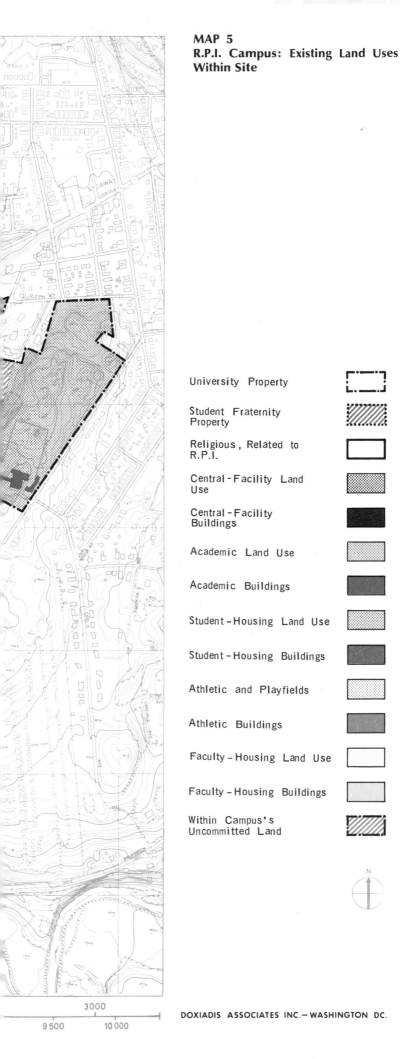

MAP 5
R.P.I. Campus: Existing Land Uses Within Site

University Property

Student Fraternity Property

Religious, Related to R.P.I.

Central-Facility Land Use

Central-Facility Buildings

Academic Land Use

Academic Buildings

Student-Housing Land Use

Student-Housing Buildings

Athletic and Playfields

Athletic Buildings

Faculty-Housing Land Use

Faculty-Housing Buildings

Within Campus's Uncommitted Land

N

3000

9 500   10 000

DOXIADIS ASSOCIATES INC.— WASHINGTON DC.

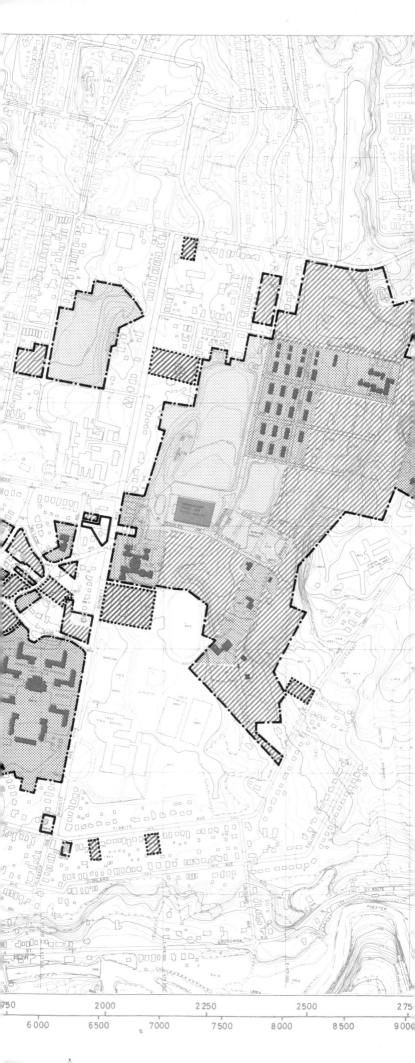

this part of the campus, wide-open spaces appear between the buildings, leaving some areas totally uncommitted as far as land use is concerned. The central portion of campus land, that of the scattered properties between Fifteenth Street and Burdett Avenue, is noted as student housing, but also presently contains an important central function that is a meeting place for all the students and faculty, the Rensselaer Union building.

Some vital statistics and comparisons of land utilization within the R.P.I. campus with those of other university campuses are shown below. (*See Table 1.*) It is of some importance to note the low built-up ratio in the academic and student-housing areas on the R.P.I. campus. This indicates the extremely wide-open spaces existing between buildings.

The academic diversification of R.P.I. is notable for a school that began by teaching «the application of science to the common purposes of life» a little over 100 years ago. Today, R.P.I. offers twenty-four educational programs leading to appropriate baccalaureate and advanced degrees. R.P.I. is primarily composed of five schools: Architecture; Engineering; Humanities and Social Sciences; Management; and Physical, Mathematical, and Life Sciences. Some of the schools are composed of smaller academic units.

Two more aspects of the composition of R.P.I.'s academic programs are relevant here. The University has a required physical-education program in order to develop habits conducive to health and to cultivate ideals of sportsmanship. The required physical-education classes introduce the students to a variety of athletic skills in their first two years of study. In cooperation with the Department of Defense, R.P.I. also offers its students, on an optional basis, military-science courses in order that they may qualify upon graduating for reserve commissions in the armed forces.

This brief examination of the organizational structure of R.P.I. would not be complete without mention of the direct relationship of the University to some outside academic and research affiliates, such as the Rensselaer Polytechnic Institute of Connecticut, known as the Hartford Graduate Center; the Hudson-Mohawk Association of Colleges and Universities; and the college programs affiliated to other institutions, such as the Biomedical Program in collaboration with Albany Medical School.

TABLE 1

Comparison of Land Utilization Within R.P.I. Campus with Those of Other University Campuses

School	Number of Students	Number of Students in Campus Housing	Acres	Number of Students per Acre	Built-Up Ratio in Academic Area	Built-Up Ratio in Student-Housing Area
M.I.T.	7,764	2,314	129.2	60	60.0	95.0
California Institute of Technology	1,490	700	80.0	19	16.0	25.0
University of Pittsburgh	22,601	3,149	111.0	200	28.8	63.0
Cornell University	13,954	4,780	730.0	20		
R.P.I.	4,954	2,190	246.0	20	13.3	11.6

The contemporary stage of development of R.P.I. began in the decade after World War II. Since then, the undergraduate enrollment has shown a modest growth, leveling off during the middle 1950's to 3,000, and has continued maintaining this upper limit into the early 1960's. (*See Table 2.*) Since that time, both undergraduate and graduate enrollment has again shown rapid growth. This may be attributed to the emphasis, on a national scale, on science and technology, the good reputation of certain of the R.P.I. undergraduate and graduate programs, the excellence of the newly available educational and research facilities, and the increasing demand by students for a professional education.

The academic load of each student consists of required and elective courses measured in credit hours. The average full-time undergraduate at R.P.I. carries 33.1 credit hours per academic year, about 17 credit hours per semester. The average full-time graduate student carries 17.4 credit hours per academic year, about 9 credit hours per semester. An academic unit is obliged each term to offer a number of

TABLE 2
Total Student Enrollment
(Actual)

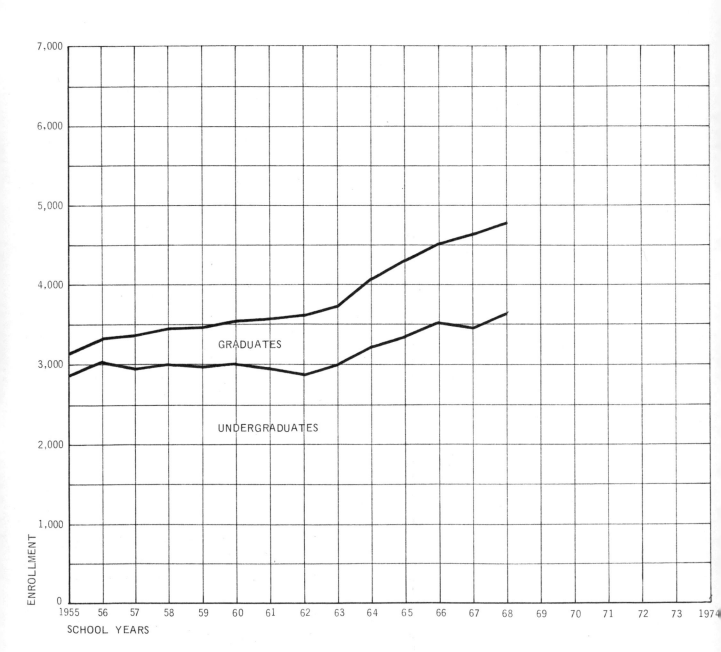

student credit hours due to student demand. The total number of student credit hours offered by each discipline is the academic load of the unit.

With regard to the academic load in different disciplines, a certain uneven pattern is noted. R.P.I. was always known in the past for the exceptional quality of its engineering education. Today, it is still renowned for this. Therefore, one should not be surprised to see more students enrolling in Engineering courses and in Physical and Life Sciences courses. (*See Table 3.*)

TABLE 3

1967-68 Distribution of Undergraduate and Graduate Student Credit Hours by Major Discipline

Discipline	Undergraduate Student Credit Hours	Graduate Student Credit Hours
Architecture	5,300	200
Engineering	23,100	8,100
Humanities	11,100	700
Management	6,000	2,500
Mathematics	17,900	3,100
Physical and life sciences	34,700	5,000
Social sciences	14,100	400
Total	112,200	20,000

R.P.I.: THE PHYSICAL PLANT

The term physical plant is meant to include all structures and networks vital to the operation of R.P.I. Naturally, there is an order of importance in the buildings comprising an educational institution. Building units used for academic purposes are of primary importance. For this reason chiefly, all discussions on the physical plant will begin with this group of buildings.

The western part of the campus between Eighth and Fifteenth streets primarily contains academic buildings, except for such structures as the Gymnasium (No. 71), some student dormitories (Nos. 59, 60, and 62), the Fifteenth Street Lounge (No. 35), the Infirmary (No. 33), the Sage Dining Hall (No. 39), the Pittsburgh Building housing the University administration (No. 31), and the Service Building (No. 37). (*See Map 6.*) In the past, all of R.P.I. was contained in this area alone, which explains the diversity of the building uses in this sector.

The central area, which is delimited by Fifteenth Street and Burdett Avenue, contains student-housing buildings, most of them constructed fairly recently, and the Rensselaer Union, the hub of social activity on the campus. The eastern section of the campus contains a few academic structures, such as those for the Nuclear Engineering and Science Building (No. 11), the Linear Accelerator Building (No. 2), and others that, perhaps, because of the nature of the work performed in them, need to be isolated in open spaces. Here, also at some distance, stands Rensselaerwyck (No. 64), temporary housing erected during World War II; this should be demolished in the near future.

The north-east end section of the campus has some very attractive housing for married students (No. 65), well sited and with a good view of the Hudson Valley. The Field House is also located in this area (No. 72), the only facility on the campus capable of seating a large audience, preferably to view athletic events rather than the performing arts.

One of the last groups of buildings comprising the R.P.I. physical plant is staff and faculty housing. These are a relatively unimportant part of the campus structure. R.P.I. does not generally provide faculty housing, nor do its plans for the future include this. Other houses that R.P.I. has acquired are of marginal quality and, since they will be removed in the near future, will not be included in subsequent detailed descriptions of the physical plant.

The R.P.I. campus consists of buildings currently in use, most of which have become or are becoming obsolete with respect to current use, adaptability to other uses, quality of facilities, location cost of maintenance and renovation, and aesthetics. The age of the structures presently comprising the R.P.I. campus is shown below. (*See Map 7.*) The age of some non-University buildings in the immediate vicinity of the campus is also shown, since they may be on the critical path of development of the future campus. The pattern of recent construction on the campus in connection with the areas containing older buildings may be noted.

Upon consideration of the curricula offered at R.P.I., the method of recording academic loads, and, finally, the «format» of the facilities inventory, a method for presenting the space allocation of the academic and research facilities was determined. The spaces assigned to each discipline were divided into four groups: offices, class laboratories, nonclass laboratories, and support spaces.

The first group, offices, includes offices for faculty members and faculty administration, i.e., spaces with «type of room code»* such as office, office service, conference room, and conference-room service. The second group, class laboratories, includes all the instructional laboratories, i.e., spaces with «type of room code» such as class laboratory, class-laboratory service, drawing room, and drawing-room service. The third group, nonclass laboratories, includes all the research laboratories, i.e., spaces with «type of room code» such as nonclass laboratory, nonclass-laboratory service, data-process-computer facility, and data-process-computer-facility service. The fourth group, support spaces, includes all spaces with «type of room code» such as stack space, study-stack space, library processing rooms, library service, exhibition, and exhibition-facility service.

The procedure for grouping the spaces by «type» — such as offices, class laboratories, nonclass laboratories, and support spaces — and by «assignment» to academic discipline was outlined above. The tabulation of the room-by-room facilities-inventory data resulted in the total net floor area used by each major discipline in the four categories of spaces.** (*See Table 4.*)

TABLE 4

1967-68 Total Net Floor Area per Major Academic Discipline in Offices, Class and Nonclass Laboratories, and Support Spaces
(In Square Feet)

Discipline	Offices	Class Laboratories	Nonclass Laboratories	Support Spaces	Total
Architecture	6,100	21,000	1,500		28,600
Engineering	33,200	59,400	78,600	1,300	172,500
Humanities	6,800	300		700	7,800
Management	5,700		400		6,100
Mathematics	8,200		3,200	900	12,300
Physical and life sciences	33,400	44,400	72,600	5,300	155,700
Social sciences	3,700	2,200	200		6,100
Total	97,100	127,300	156,500	8,200	389,100

The initial tabulation of the inventory into the four groups of spaces was completed with a remaining fifth group of spaces. This group had a «type of room» classification titled «general assignment,»*** and, as the title indicates, these spaces are not assigned to any one academic unit. This is the pool of class-rooms, and a few drawing rooms, that are used by all disciplines interchangeably for lectures, recitation, discussion, and drawing-design. The general-assignment group includes ninety-seven rooms of various sizes, with a total net area of 87,300 square feet. The total capacity of these rooms, measured in student seats or stations, is 6,446.

To conclude this description of the academic facilities of R.P.I., the University Library, the most important member of the academic family, must be mentioned. It is now housed in a recently acquired chapel, a structure unsuitable for a library. A summary breakdown of its present facilities, expressed in net floor area, is as follows:

---

* The data were furnished on punched cards, using IBM 29 standard code-punching and a uniform code for all organizational units.

** Total net floor area is approximately 30-40 per cent less than total floor area.

*** It is assumed that all classrooms, drawing rooms, and so on, not included by «symbol» in the general-assignment category are of a special use and, therefore, have been counted as class laboratories.

MAP 6
R.P.I. Campus: Facilities Available in 1968

ACADEMIC FACILITIES

ARCHITECTURE	GREENE BLDG.	1
	LINEAR ACCELERATOR	2
	NORTH HALL BLDG.	3
	RICKETTS BLDG.	4
	SAGE BLDG.	5
	HYPERSONIC LAB. BLDG.	6
ENGINEERING	BLAW KNOX I	7
	TROY BLDG.	8
	MATERIAL RESEARCH BLDG.	9
	ENG. SCIENCE BLDG.	10
	NUCL. ENG. & SCIENCE BLDG.	11
HUMANITIES	WEST HALL BLDG.	12
	PEOPLES AVENUE COMPLEX C.D.	13
MANAGEMENT	MANAGEMENT BLDG.	14
MATHEMATICS	AMOS EATON BLDG.	15
	BLAW KNOX II	16
	OBSERVATORY BLDG.	17
	SEISMOGRAPH BLDG.	18
	PILOT STRUCTURE	19
PHYS. & LIFE SCIENCES	WALKER BLDG.	20
	MASON HOUSE	21
	SCIENCE CENTER	22
	CHEM. RES. BLDG. (UNDER CONST.)	23
SOCIAL SCIENCES	PSYCHOLOGY LABORATORY	24
	PEOPLES AVENUE COMPLEX D.	25
GEN. ASSIGNMENT SPACES	CARNEGIE BLDG.	26
LIBRARY	LIBRARY BLDG. (CHAPEL)	27
ROTC	WINSLOW BLDG.	28

CENTRAL FACILITIES

PITTSBURG BLDG.	31
RENSSELAER UNION	32
INFIRMARY	33
POLICE	34
15th ST. LOUNGE	35
BOILER HOUSE	36
SERVICE BLDG.	37
STUDENT AFFAIRS	38
FACULTY DINING HALL	39
GREENHOUSE	40
CENTREX	41

STUDENT HOUSING

	BRAY HALL	51
	CARY HALL	52
	CROCKETT HALL	53
	HALL HALL	54
FRESHMEN	NASON HALL	55
	WARREN HALL	56
	DINING HALL	57
	NEW DORMITORIES (UNDER CONST.)	58
	CHURCH SIX	59
	CHURCH BUCK COOPER	
	McDONALD, ROEBLING, PARDEE,	
UPPER CLASSMEN	CALDWELL, HUNT, WHITE,	60
	BURDETT RESIDENCE HALLS	61
	CASSAT OLEMENT HIRAI	
	WHAITE HEARNE VOORHEES	62
	AUXILIARY DORMS 2,3,4	63
MARRIED	RENSSELAERWYCK	64
STUDENTS	BRYCKWYCK	65

STAFF HOUSING

RESIDENCE	70

ATHLETICS

GYMNASIUM	71
FIELD HOUSE	72

NOTE : THE EXISTING ACADEMIC BUILDINGS HAVE BEEN GROUPED ACCORDING TO THEIR PREDOMINANT USERS

University Property

Student Fraternity Property

Religious, Related to R.P.I.

N

3000

9 500   10 000

DOXIADIS ASSOCIATES INC.— WASHINGTON DC.

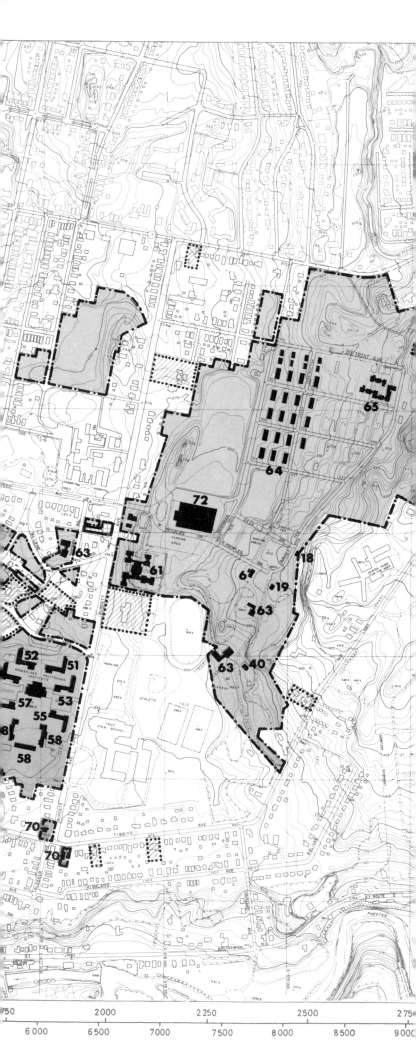

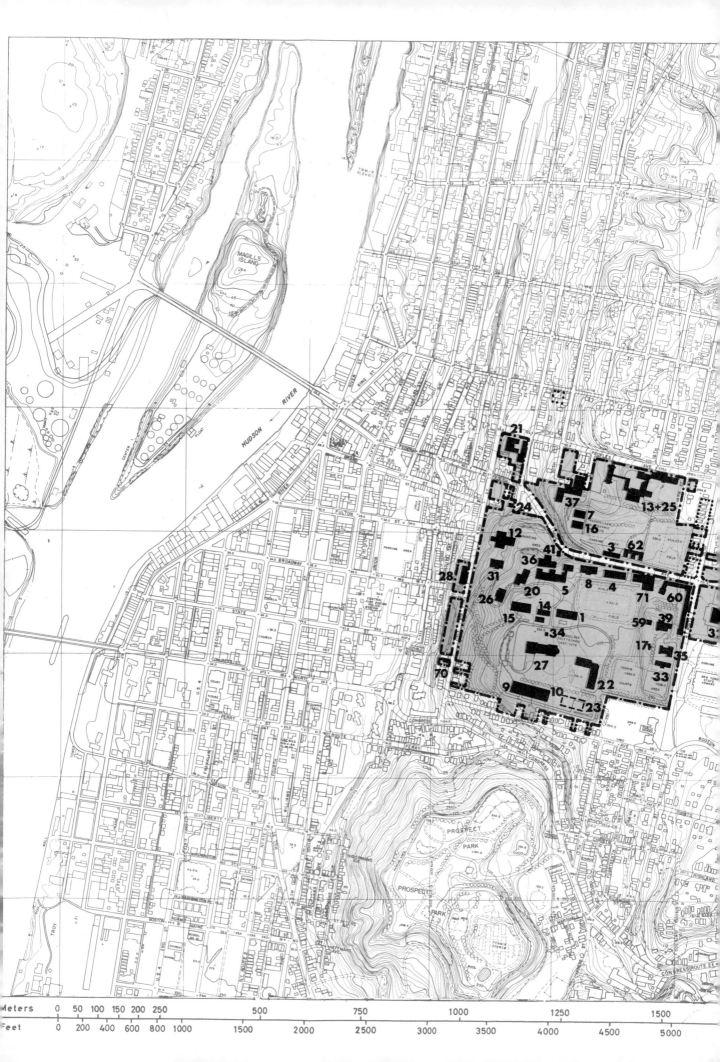

MAP 7
R.P.I. Campus: Age of Buildings

University Property	
Student Fraternity Property	
Religious, Related to R.P.I.	
Structures Not Belonging to R.P.I.	
Erected Prior to 1920	
Erected Between 1920 - 29	
Erected Between 1930 - 39	
Erected Between 1940 - 49	
Erected Between 1950 - 59	
Erected After 1960	

Note : Two colors on a building indicate initial construction and subsequent remodeling

N

DOXIADIS ASSOCIATES INC.— WASHINGTON DC.

3000

9 500   10 000

DETROIT AVE

RENSSELAER
POLYTECHNIC
INSTITUTE

PARKING
AREA

ATHLETIC   FIELD

TIBBITS   AVE

HIGHLAND   AVE

BRUNSWICK   RD.

POESTEN

1750   2000   2250   2500   2750

6000   6500   7000   7500   8000   8500   9000

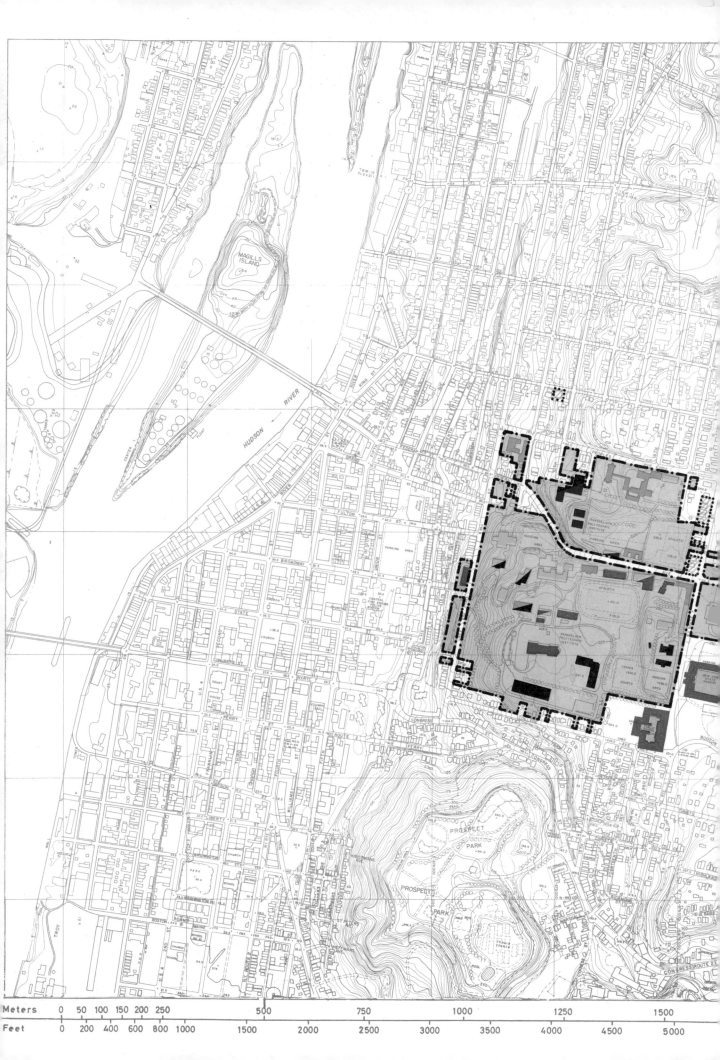

MAGILLS ISLAND

HUDSON RIVER

RENSSELAER POLYTECHNIC INSTITUTE

PROSPECT PARK

PROSPECT PARK

Meters	0	50	100	150	200	250		500		750		1000		1250		1500
Feet	0	200	400	600	800	1000		1500		2000		2500		3000		3500		4000		4500		5000

	PHYSICAL AND LIFE SCIENCES		SOCIAL SCIENCES		ROTC		TOTAL		
Number of Class Hours per Week	Per Cent of Class Hours per Week	Number of Class Hours per Week	Per Cent of Class Hours per Week	Number of Class Hours per Week	Per Cent of Class Hours per Week	Number of Class Hours per Week	Per Cent of Class Hours per Week	Existing [a] Rooms
5	0.9					38.5	2.2	
6	12.1	9	5.4			166	9.5	
	5.1	20	12.0			202.5	11.6	④
	12.5	18	10.9	3	10.4	232	13.2	②
	32.0	12	7.2	6	20.7	269	15.4	⑥
	5.8	17	10.3	8	27.6	241.5	13.8	⑫
	5.6	18	10.9	3	10.4	117	6.7	⑪
	4.1	9	5.4	0.5	1.7	85	4.8	⑨
	3.1	6	3.6	2	6.9	74	4.2	⑦
	1.3	9	5.4			46	2.6	⑥
	0.2	18	10.9	0.5	1.7	38	2.2	④
	2.0	3	1.8	2	6.9	36	2.1	⑤
	3.0	3	1.8	1	3.4	22	1.3	④
	0.2					29	1.7	②
	2.0	6	3.6			25	1.4	③
	0.5	9	5.4			33	1.9	③
	1.5	3	1.8			14	0.8	
	1.5					13	0.7	①
	1.5	6	3.6			15	0.9	
	0.8					6	0.3	⑥
	0.8'			3	10.3	25	1.4	③
	1.0					8	0.5	④
	1.0					5	0.3	②
	0.5					3	0.2	
	1.0					5	0.3	②
	100.0	166	100.0	29	100.0	1,748.5	100.0	

DOXIADIS ASSOCIATES INC. — WASHINGTON DC.

Row Number	Room-Size and Class Hour-Size Groups (number of seats/students)	ARCHITECTURE		ENGINEERING		HUMANITIES		MANAGEMENT		MATHEMATICS	
		Number of Class Hours per Week	Per Cent of Class Hours per Week	Number of Class Hours per Week	Per Cent of Class Hours per Week	Number of Class Hours per Week	Per Cent of Class Hours per Week	Number of Class Hours per Week	Per Cent of Class Hours per Week	Number of Class Hours per Week	Per Cent of Class Hours per Week
1	5 or less			28	6.8	4	1.5			3	1.1
2	6-10	1	2.0	43.5	10.6	43	15.8	15	9.9	7	2.5
3	11-15			66	16.1	48	17.6	28.5	18.9	20	7.2
4	16-20			46	11.3	58	21.3	22	14.6	36	12.9
5	21-25	5	10.3	32	7.8	27	9.9	21	13.9	40	14.4
6	26-30	18.5	38.3	40	9.8	32	11.8	21	13.9	82	29.4
7	31-35	6	12.3	25	6.1	30	11.1	2	1.4	11	3.9
8	36-40	4	8.2	21.5	5.3	12	4.4	13	8.6	9	3.2
9	41-45	4.5	9.4	15.5	3.8	9	3.3	5	3.5	20	7.2
10	46-50			17	4.1	6	2.2			9	3.2
11	51-55	3.5	7.2	12	2.9	3	1.1				
12	56-60	6	12.3	8	1.9			9	5.9		
13	61-65			3	0.8					3	1.1
14	66-70			13	3.2			6	3.9	9	3.2
15	71-75			11	2.7						
16	76-80			10	2.5					12	4.3
17	81-85			2	0.5					3	1.1
18	86-90			1	0.2					6	2.1
19	91-95			3	0.8						
20	96-100			3	0.8						
21	101-150			5	1.2			8	5.5	6	2.1
22	151-200			1	0.2					3	1.1
23	201-250			1	0.2						
24	251-300			1	0.2						
25	301 or more			1	0.2						
26	TOTAL	48.5	100.0	409.5	100.0	272	100.0	150.5	100.0	279	100.0

[a] Numbers in circles are number of rooms for each size category.

Offices	4,600 sq. ft.
Storage and Stack Spaces	24,000 sq. ft.
Support Spaces	4,800 sq. ft.

An attempt was made to analyze the utilization of the five types of spaces (offices, class laboratories, nonclass laboratories, support spaces, and classrooms) by different academic disciplines. Limits of the data, in addition to the inherent character of some of the spaces themselves, made the task impossible in some cases.

The large floor area allocated by each school at R.P.I. to faculty offices is difficult to analyze. Perhaps one of the main reasons is that each of the schools uses some buildings that have been converted to academic use. The adaptability of some of these buildings to serve current needs is, in some cases, questionable. As a result, an awkward corner on the floor plan of a converted building easily becomes an «office.» Another reason for a high percentage of net floor area assigned to office use is, perhaps, the need to give desks to some of the graduate assistants.

The second category of spaces whose utilization is difficult to analyze is the group of spaces labeled nonclass laboratories. Basically, this group of spaces includes all the research laboratories dispersed in the different buildings of the R.P.I. physical plant. There is no set pattern for utilizing research spaces. The variables controlling the demand for these spaces are, for instance, fashions, student and faculty desires, government- and industry-sponsored research, and so on. These factors vary from year to year.

Another category of spaces presenting difficulties in the analysis of their utilization are the support spaces. These are usually the leftover spaces in rehabilitated buildings, rather than actually planned needs for storage rooms or stack areas. The utilization analysis was, therefore, limited to classrooms and class laboratories. For these two categories enough data were available for certain patterns to emerge.

In general, the level of average weekly utilization of classrooms that is actually attainable is substantially lower than that for the entire scheduled week, which for R.P.I. is a 45-hour maximum. How much lower than the maximum is dependent upon factors such as the proportion of laboratory instruction in the curriculum; campus-wide scheduling of classes, rather than scheduling by schools or departments; schedule conflicts due to crossover courses (engineers taking courses in other schools), and so on.

Data is provided above for the distribution of rooms and classes (i.e., class meeting hours) by size category and by academic units. (*See Table 5.*) This distribution determines the Station Utilization Index, i.e., how full classrooms are when they are in use. The current imbalance between the size distribution of classroom demand and the distribution by sizes of the classroom supply is indicated below. (*See Table 6.*) This lack of «fit» indicates an inefficient use of large rooms by small classes because enough smaller rooms are not available. The supply of classroom hours has been plotted in terms of the existing scheduling, which varies from 9 to 24.5 hours per week.

Laboratories include all instructional rooms involving special designs or facilities of a kind or degree that make them particularly serviceable for instruction in a single course or a group of related courses. With respect to classrooms, a chair is considered as a student station. In laboratories, the definition is not so simple. In most cases, a laboratory station can be identified with the area of facilities required for a student to carry out his work under the instructional program of the course. Thus, a student station may be a length of chemistry bench, the area around a piece of demonstration equipment, or a drafting table. In some circumstances, the number of stations in a laboratory (i.e., its capacity) may vary with the particular course being taught, with the particular experiment being conducted, or with the availability of faculty to supervise student work.

Whereas a classroom can equally well be scheduled for courses in mathematics, history, or economics, laboratories are generally not interchangeable, so that surplus capacity in biology laboratories cannot be used to schedule overflow loads in physics. Because of this basic heterogeneity, it is not possible to summarize utilization data in terms of averages.

In addition to the specific limitation on laboratory utilization because of design, there are some additional constraints, such as schedule problems, staff limitations, nonscheduled use, and small enrollments. The last two constraints may need an explanation. The nonscheduled use of laboratories is the use for make-up work at the end of laboratory sessions and the like; many laboratories may also require significant time for setting up before, and cleaning up after, the sessions.

The problem with the utilization of some of the class laboratories at R.P.I., however, lies in small enrollments. Once it has been decided to offer a specialized course requiring a special laboratory facility and the laboratory has been provided, the attainable utilization of the laboratory is limited not by room size or by schedule problems but by small enrollments. The distribution of forty-seven class laboratories among three disciplines — Engineering, Physical and Life Sciences, and Social Sciences — is shown below. (*See Table 7.*) It can be noted that only 16 laboratories were used about 16 hours or more, which is the approximate equivalent of five days a week of afternoon use.

About 40 per cent of the total student population of R.P.I. live on the campus; the rest live in

TABLE 6
Classroom Supply and Demand Distribution by Size Categories
(Spring, 1968)

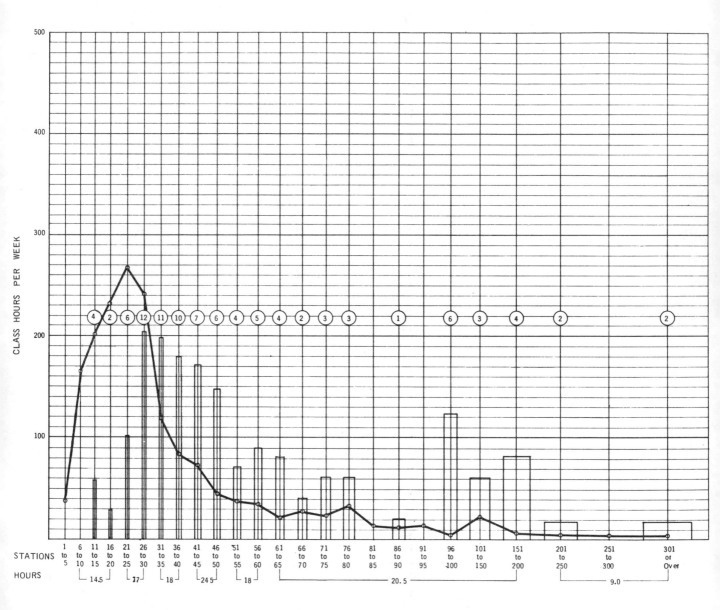

Note :

Demand in class hours per week
by class-size intervals

Number of rooms for each size category
where width of bar proportionate to
classroom capacity

DOXIADIS ASSOCIATES INC. — WASHINGTON DC.

fraternities and off-campus facilities, varying from rooms rented in private houses to private apartments and houses in the city of Troy and neighboring townships. *(See Map 8.)* The largest concentration of single-men student housing appears to be in the area of the freshmen dormitories — a complex of seven older buildings and three under construction. The first group, the old buildings, consists of six three-story dormitories with dining facilities centrally located. The second group, the three new buildings, south of the first, consists of three four-story dormitories for male students. This group contains a few more amenities than the first, such as small lounges, special rooms for listening to music, laundry facilities, and so on.

The Quadrangle dormitories, the second large concentration of single-men students (Nos. 59 and 60), are part of campus tradition, built on the row-house principle. The buildings are situated very near an important intersection; a decision with regard to intersection improvement may require the buildings' removal in the future.

TABLE 7

Distribution of Class Laboratory Rooms
by Frequency of Schedule Use in Hours per Week and by Faculty
(Spring, 1968)

Row Number	Hours per Week of Scheduled Laboratory Utilization	ENGINEERING		PHYSICAL & LIFE SCIENCES		SOCIAL SCIENCES		TOTAL		
		Number	Per Cent	Number	Per Cent	Number	Per Cent	Number	Per Cent	Cumulative Per Cent
1	0- 3	8	40	6	23.2			14	29.8	29.8
2	4- 6	3	15	3	11.6			6	12.8	42.6
3	7- 9			1	3.8	1	100	2	4.3	46.9
4	10-12	2	10	3	11.6			5	10.6	57.5
5	13-15			4	15.4			4	8.5	66.0
6	16-18	1	5	2	7.6			3	6.4	72.4
7	19-21	2	10	2	7.6			4	8.5	80.9
8	22-24	2	10	3	11.6			5	10.6	91.5
9	25-27			1	3.8			1	2.1	93.6
10	28-30	2	10	1	3.8			3	6.4	100.0
11	31-33									
12	Total	20	100	26	100.0	1	100	47	100.0	

The new Burdett Residence Halls (No. 61) provide adequate and congenial spaces for living and recreation in an atmosphere conducive to study. The building was designed on the principle of four wings attached to a nucleus of common facilities such as dining area, lounges, and so on. The isolated wing design provides flexibility for assigning such an area to women students. The single-men dormitory structure (the «E» building) facing the western part of Sage Avenue (No. 62) is one of the older dormitories of the R.P.I. campus and is built on a variation of the principle of the Quadrangle dormitories.

Lastly, there are three auxiliary dormitories (No. 63) erected on R.P.I. property. These buildings are rented to student fraternities. One of them is located on Sherry Road, and two on the extension of Sunset Drive at the eastern part of the campus. Vital statistics for all buildings in the category of student housing for single men are shown below. *(See Table 8.)*

Many universities in the United States inherited a number of temporary units from government agencies after World War II (No. 64). R.P.I. also has on its property 172 of these apartment-type units. Presently, these units are occupied by married students. This housing is today considered substandard and will be removed by the University within a short time.

New residence units for married students have recently been built (No. 65). The buildings are located at the northeastern corner of the campus, lying on a slope that affords each apartment a fine view of the Hudson Valley. The units are designed to fulfill the varying needs of married students. There are 53 such units operating at present. The net floor area of the buildings is 34,500 square feet, which indicates that the average unit has an area of about 640 square feet.

TABLE 8
Vital Statistics for All Buildings in Category
of Student Housing for Single Men

Unit	Student Capacity	Net Floor Area (in square feet)	Net Floor Area per Student
Freshman housing [a]	920	164,700 [b]	180
Quadrangle dormitories	350	57,000	160
Burdett residence halls	218	49,600 [b]	225
«E» building	122	15,600	130
Auxiliary dormitories	112	26,200 [b]	235
Total	1,722	313,100	

[a] Does not include units under construction.
[b] Includes dining facilities.

About 1,000 students live in student fraternities. The fraternity houses are dispersed in many structures around the present campus and at various locations throughout the city. A few fraternities have built new structures designed for their needs, but the majority are located in converted residences and thus have inherited all the problems of the home-owners in the vicinity around the campus — namely, deterioration, congestion, and high taxes.

Approximately another 1,000 students live in off-campus housing, using a local or Tri-City Area address. The housing market in Troy is very poor and will continue to deteriorate in the immediate future. This may force R.P.I. to consider providing more housing not only for single men, but also for married students.

Certain facilities are labeled as central, such as those housing the extracurricular activities of R.P.I. students. To this central group also belong the service facilities for the operation of the campus. The student facilities devoted to extracurricular activities are the Fifteenth Street Lounge, the Field House, and the recreational spaces of the Rensselaer Union building. The Fifteenth Street Lounge has a seating capacity of about 200 persons for theatrical performances given by the R.P.I. Players. Since the floor is level, a clear view of the stage is difficult, however. The Field House is designed for organized athletic events and is, therefore, unsuitable for performing-arts programs, with the exception of some spectacular musicals, such as ice-skating shows. The Rensselaer Union building, in the absence of other facilities, has become the hub of social and recreational activities on the campus. Its television rooms, lounges, and bowling alleys are intensively used by R.P.I. students.

As service facilities on the campus, one may classify Pittsburgh Building, which houses almost all the University's administrative units and is located at an inaccessible site within the campus; the Student Affairs building, on Sage Avenue, which is an old converted residence; the Infirmary, an old prefabricated structure serving temporarily as a student infirmary; the Service Building, facing Peoples Avenue, designed to house all the maintenance and service shops, including the University receiving depot; and, finally, the Boiler House, located on the northwestern part of the campus and inadequate to handle the needs of the expanding campus.

The present gymnasium is now obsolete for most types of intercollegiate, intramural athletic activities and recreational use. It is well below minimum standards for other sports and is inadequate to serve the present and growing campus population. The number of women students is increasing, and no provision for their athletic and recreational interests is available. There is a notable absence of playfields in readily available locations on the R.P.I. campus. South of the present gymnasium is the football field, available only for intercollegiate activities.

At some distance from the gymnasium and the dormitories are baseball and practice fields. What is obviously missing from the R.P.I. campus is not so much fields for organized sports but a dispersion of playfields and tennis courts within the dormitory areas for recreational use by the student who can get away from his books for only a short time.

A brief description of the networks, pedestrian and vehicular, connecting the units that comprise the campus is required in order to complete the discussion on the R.P.I. physical plant. The pattern of pedestrian movement within and around the property that comprises the present campus is shown below. *(See Map 9.)*

MAP 8
R.P.I. Campus: Location and Quantity of Students Housed Within Campus

Bray	**51**
Cary	**52**
Crockett	**53**
Hall	**54**
Nason	**55**
Warren	**56**
Dining Hall (Freshmen)	**57**
New Freshmen Dormitories (Under Construction)	**58**
Church Six	**59**
Church, Buck, Cooper, McDonald, Roebling, Pardee, Caldwell Hunt, White	**60**
Burdett Residence Halls	**61**
Cassat, Clement, Hirai, Whaite, Hearne, Voorhees	**62**
Auxiliary Dormitories 2, 3, 4	**63**
Rensselaerwyck	**64**
Bryckwyck	**65**

University Property

Student Fraternity Property

Religious, Related to R.P.I.

Single Students

Married Students

1200
1000
800
600
400
200
100
50

N

DOXIADIS ASSOCIATES INC. — WASHINGTON DC.

3000

9500   10000

MAGILLS
ISLAND

HUDSON   RIVER

RENSSELAER
POLYTECHNIC
INSTITUTE

62

60

59

PROSPECT
PARK

PROSPECT
PARK

MAP 9
R.P.I. Campus: Movement of Pedestrians and Approximate Traffic Volumes

University Property

Student Fraternity Property

Religious, Related to R.P.I.

Note : Volumes are approximate

N

3000

9 500   10 000

DOXIADIS ASSOCIATES INC.— WASHINGTON DC.

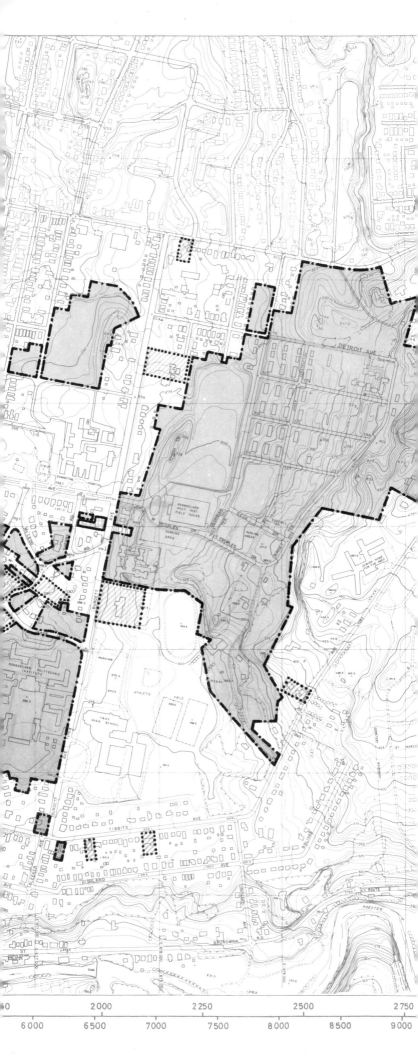

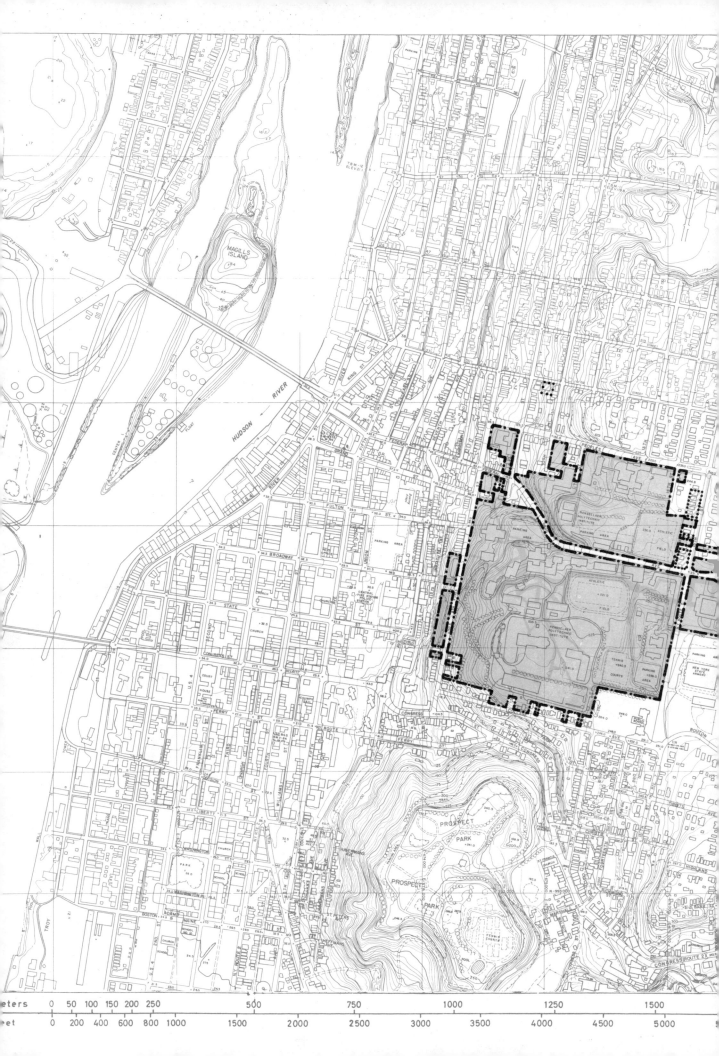

The most serious problem with regard to pedestrian traffic is the bottleneck caused by the converging of all footpaths at the crossing at Fifteenth Street and Sage Avenue. Even if crosstown automobile routes are rerouted to free Fifteenth Street, the situation will not greatly improve, for even in 1960 the reserve capacity of Fifteenth Street was almost exhausted. *(See Map 3.)* Rerouting east-west traffic presently using this street may reduce some of the traffic volume; but, since 1960, the situation has undoubtedly grown worse, and all indications for the future show a rise in automobile ownership, people's mobility, and traveling speeds.

There is no concise University road system within the campus to serve the buildings and provide staff parking at close proximity to places of instruction or employment. Parking is already critical, and increases in the staff and student population can only make it worse. With open areas rising to premium value for recreational and academic activities, large surface parking areas will be difficult to obtain in close proximity to campus facilities.

The vehicular network within the campus and the peripheral city streets used for the automobile traffic moving to and from the different University building units is shown below. *(See Map 10.)* Excluding the eastern campus parking lots, utilized only for overnight parking or parking for attending events in the Field House, the total capacity of parking areas within the main campus is about 1,000 spaces.

University Property

Student Fraternity
Property

Religious, Related to
R.P.I.

N

3000

9 500   10 000

DOXIADIS ASSOCIATES INC.— WASHINGTON DC.

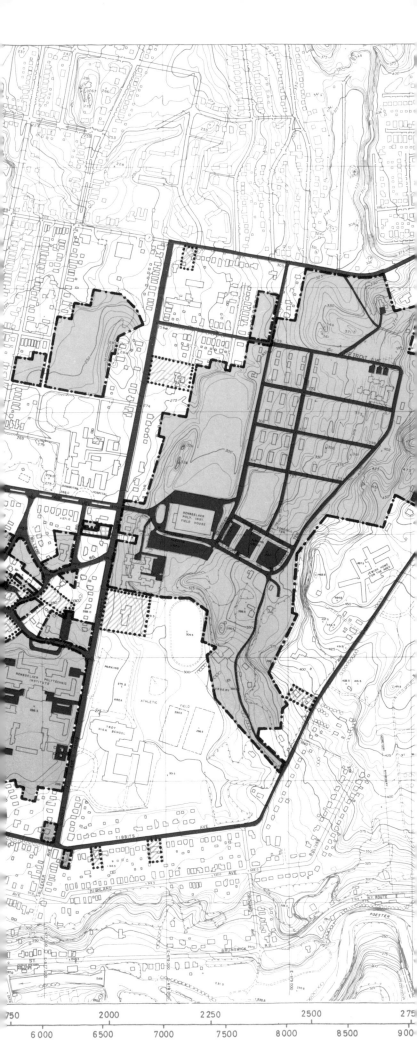

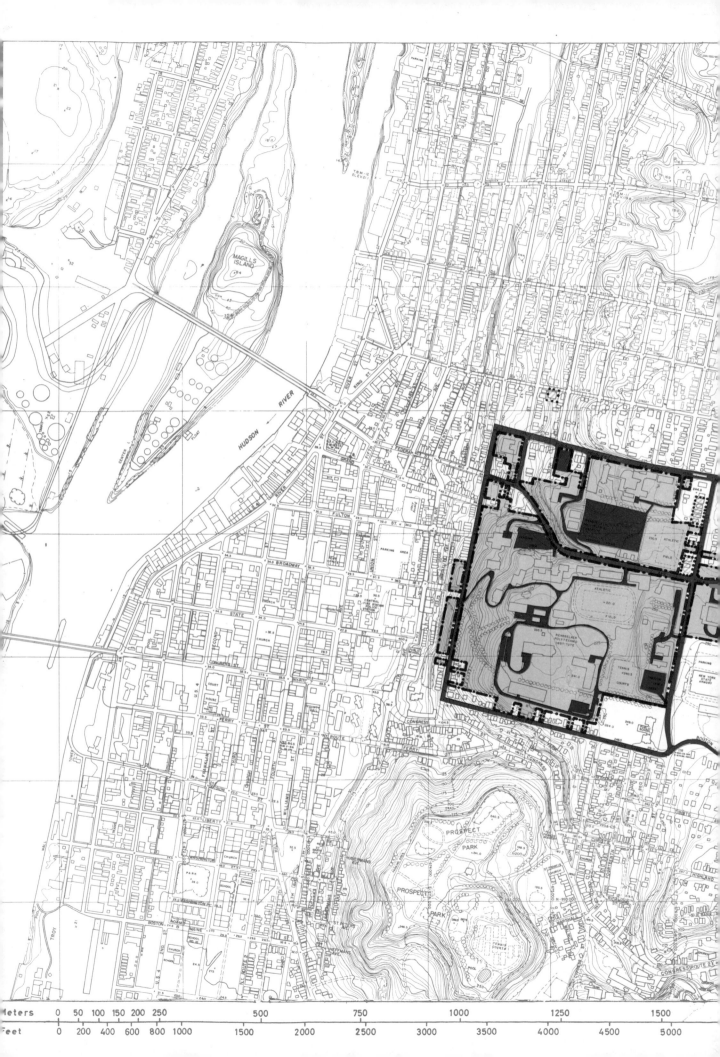

MAGILLS
ISLAND

HUDSON   RIVER

RIVER

RENSSELAER
POLYTECHNIC
INSTITUTE

ATHLETIC
FIELD

ATHLETIC
FIELD

TENNIS
COURTS

NEW YORK
STATE
ARMORY

PARKING

PROSPECT
PARK

PROSPECT

PARK

TENNIS
COURTS

TROY

Part II

PROPOSALS AND REQUIREMENTS FOR CHANGE

Chapter 2 Assumptions for Long-Range Planning

For any long-range planning a set of general assumptions are necessary in order to provide the framework for the development of the plans and programs of the assignment. This chapter contains a list of these assumptions, which were drawn up by the consultants in collaboration with the University administration. The list contains some external factors that affect the University and assumptions that, although based on these external factors, are a matter of internal forecasts.

GENERAL

According to Department of Health, Education, and Welfare figures, between 50 and 60 per cent of secondary-school graduates will presently be seeking higher education. Public higher educational facilities must be developed to meet most of the requirements of four-year graduate-program growth. The private sector will not grow as rapidly as these demands, and both the private and public sectors will begin to approach ceilings in enrollment. National demand for scientists and engineers who are educated to higher levels will continue to grow and to attract secondary-school graduates.

State and federal funds for capital purposes, for student grant and loan financial aid, and for a variety of special purposes will also continue to grow. Funds for the support of academic research on a project basis will continue to grow as well, but at a slower rate. State and federal formulas will be developed to enable general institutional grants to be made to private institutions. This will be coupled with the requirement that participating institutions join in local, regional, and national efforts in long-range planning and in interinstitutional cooperation. Uniform systems for reporting academic, financial, personnel, and physical data will be developed. These will require all institutions to maintain appropriate internal systems to provide these data.

Private institutions will continue to depend upon support from private sources within the economy and will find it necessary to increase efforts in this area if they wish to retain their special roles in society as privately controlled institutions. Large national foundations will play a lesser role, making it necessary to shift emphasis to individual gifts — particularly those of alumni — and to corporate support.

The region will become increasingly an educational, cultural, recreational, and governmental center. Changing and improving transportation systems will make the area an important distribution and communication center. Regional planning will develop in importance, with the objective of finding ways to surmount the obstacles of historical-political subdivisions in solving the common problems of the region. Universities in the area will play an increasingly influential role in the solution of these problems, individually and jointly.

CITY OF TROY

Despite a desire to attract new industries and to retain the present ones, Troy will continue to depend less and less on major business to support its economy. Urban renewal will continue to improve the central city and to slow down the flight of its residents to the suburbs and other communities, but massive internal aid will be required to provide significant amounts of low- and middle-cost housing and their supporting services. Troy will become increasingly an educational and residential community and decreasingly an industrial community.

For planning purposes, it has been assumed that, by 1990, the current efforts of the city's private and public renewal program will produce favorable results. Some of the presumed effects of the city's revitalization will be the completion of the urban-renewal projects adjacent to the R.P.I. campus and the improvement of some of the city networks. These network improvements imply the construction of the north-south arterial highway by the western boundary of R.P.I. proposed by the state of New York and the development of a contemporary city sewer network with an interceptor or a treatment plant to prevent pollution of the Hudson River.

R.P.I.

R.P.I., an important member of a growing educational community in the Tri-City Area, will continue with its transitional development to become a technological university emphasizing science and technology. It will continue as a coeducational university under private control, offering appropriate fields of study leading to baccalaureate, master's, and doctor's degrees, as well as continuing professional education to those who have completed formal study in their respective fields.

In the coming period of Troy's revitalization, R.P.I., recognizing the need for the unification of its properties, will establish boundaries for its campus growth and will avoid purchasing land for University use outside these limits. A moderate land-acquisition program within the area of interest contiguous to the existing campus will be continued. Emphasis on the growth of graduate education and research will also continue, with the objective of fully developing selected areas of excellence and of initiating programs in appropriate new areas. These will take place within the scope of the existing major disciplines described above. (*See Table 3.*)

Degree programs in the humanities and in the social sciences will continue to be developed and will assume a growing influence on, and importance for, programs in the scientific and engineering areas as more faculty members of higher caliber and broader interests are acquired. Advanced interdisciplinary areas of study, such as environmental studies and the life sciences, will be developed as they increase in importance to society. The undergraduate program in Architecture will remain a five-year program at the level of 250 students. The present two-semester plan for studies will be continued, as will the system for computing degree requirements and academic loads. The system is based on the quantity of instruction expressed in student credit hours.

With the more rapid growth of the educational community in the region, the R.P.I. undergraduate student population will continue to grow at a controlled rate of approximately 60 students per year until a ceiling of 4,500 is reached around 1985. These will be full-time students pursuing an average of approximately 33 credit hours per year. The graduate student population will continue to grow at a controlled rate of approximately 65 students per year until a ceiling of 2,500 is reached in 1989. About half of these will be part-time students pursuing 9 or less credit hours per semester. The average graduate student will carry 17.5 credit hours per year.

The R.P.I. campus consists of buildings currently in use that are or will become obsolete with respect to current usage adaptability to other uses, quality of facilities, location, cost of maintenance and renovation, and aesthetics. These buildings will be taken out of service and replaced as rapidly as new ones can be constructed or as existing structures are renovated. Other existing buildings will be renovated in order to improve their standards, to adapt them to changing program requirements, and to serve new functions.

By 1990-95 it is assumed that many existing buildings presently comprising R.P.I. will be removed. It is also assumed that general remodeling, rehabilitation, and modernization, other than major renovation of existing buildings, will continue in order to raise the functional and aesthetic standard of all facilities. By 1990 many buildings will be renovated. Some of them will also be used differently.

As the University grows and expands, it is assumed that the facilities will grow in proportion to the increase in the student population. This is not the case as a rule but, for the purpose of roughly establishing the needs of the master plan, this suggested assumption is adequate. This proposition assumes not only the same density of utilization for all the facilities in the future, but also that the University, the different schools, and all the academic units are satisfied with present conditions; thus, for establishing future needs, the present allocated spaces are increased proportionately. But this is not the case at R.P.I.; therefore, a correction for the inadequacies of present facilities will be necessary.

Chapter 3 Building Requirements

This chapter tries to determine the floor areas needed by the components of the physical plant for the proposed master plan. The projection of needs has been based on the assumption that the increase of the physical facilities will be in proportion to the growth of the student population.

ACADEMIC FACILITIES

The academic facilities will increase in proportion to the academic load generated by the student population. This generated load is usually expressed in student credit hours. The academic facilities are composed of three groups of spaces: the spaces assigned to academic disciplines (offices, class laboratories, nonclass laboratories, and support spaces), the general-assignment spaces (classrooms), and the spaces constituting the University Library.

Three methods will be used for projecting building requirements. The projections for the spaces assigned to academic disciplines will be based on student credit hours; the projections for classrooms will be based on classroom contact hours; and the University Library, since it is a special problem, will be treated differently — its requirements will be based on a rough standard, varying with the size and type of total student enrollment.

The distribution of actual student credit hours by major discipline for 1967-68 and the forecasts made by R.P.I.'s Office of Academic Planning for future years are shown below. (*See Tables 9-11.*) The distribution of weighted student credit hours by major discipline is also shown and is based on the assumption that weighted student credit hours are equal to undergraduate student credit hours plus three times graduate student credit hours. The actual classroom contact hours for the fall term of 1967-68 (in

TABLE 9

Distribution of Undergraduate Student Credit Hours by Major Discipline

| Discipline | 1967-68 | | 1980 | 1980-81 | 1989 and After |
	Student Credit Hours	Per Cent of Total	Per Cent of Total	Total	Total
Architecture	5,300			5,000	5,000
Engineering	23,100	21	18	24,000	26,000
Humanities	11,100	11	15	20,000	21,000
Management	6,000	6	8	10,000	11,000
Mathematics	17,900	17	15	20,000	21,000
Physical and life sciences	34,700	32	29	39,000	41,000
Social sciences	14,100	13	15	20,000	21,000
Total	112,200	100	100	138,000	146,000

TABLE 10

Distribution of Graduate Student Credit Hours by Major Discipline

| Discipline | 1967-68 | | 1980 | 1980-81 | 1989 and After |
	Student Credit Hours	Per Cent of Total	Per Cent of Total	Total	Total
Architecture	200	1	2	700	900
Engineering	8,100	40	37	12,400	16,100
Humanities	700	4	6	2,000	2,600
Management	2,500	13	15	5,000	6,500
Mathematics	3,100	15	14	4,600	6,000
Physical and life sciences	5,000	25	22	7,500	9,600
Social sciences	400	2	4	1,400	1,800
Total	20,000	100	100	33,600	43,500

TABLE 11

Distribution of Weighted Student Credit Hours by Major Discipline

| Discipline | 1967-68 | | 1980-81 | | 1989 and After | |
	Total	Per Cent of Total	Total	Per Cent of Total	Total	Per Cent of Total
Architecture	6,000	3	7,000	3	8,000	3
Engineering	47,000	28	61,000	26	74,000	27
Humanities	13,000	7	26,000	11	29,000	11
Management	14,000	8	25,000	10	30,000	11
Mathematics	27,000	16	34,000	14	39,000	14
Physical and life sciences	50,000	29	61,000	26	70,000	25
Social sciences	15,000	9	24,000	10	26,000	9
Total	172,000	100	238,000	100	276,000	100

TABLE 12

Classroom Contact Hours
(Fall Term)

Program	1967-68	1980-81	1989 and After
Graduate	6,900	11,400	14,800
Undergraduate	51,600	62,800	66,400
Total	58,500	74,200	81,200

one week's cycle) and the forecasts made by R.P.I.'s Office for Academic Planning for future years are shown above. *(See Table 12.)* The term «classroom contact hours» can be best explained by an example: The count of classroom contact hours of twenty students meeting at one time in a classroom for a two-hour lecture is forty.

The projections of student credit hours and classroom contact hours are used for establishing future building requirements in terms of space assigned to academic disciplines (offices, class laboratories, nonclass laboratories, support spaces) and the general-assignment spaces (classrooms). The method is outlined below with an example. The office-space projections utilize the *weighted* student credit hours for each discipline. For example, the requirements of the Physical and Life Sciences are computed as follows:

$$\text{Credit hours per square foot} = \frac{\text{1967-68 student credit hours}}{\text{Existing office space}}$$
$$= \frac{50,000}{33,400} = 1.50$$

$$\text{1980-81 requirements} = \frac{\text{1980-81 student credit hours}}{\text{Credit hours per square foot}}$$
$$= \frac{61,000}{1.5} = 41,000 \text{ square feet}$$

For the other three spaces assigned to academic disciplines — i.e., class laboratories, nonclass laboratories, and support spaces — the following types of student credit hours are utilized for establishing future building requirements. Class laboratories are basically an undergraduate facility; therefore, undergraduate student credit hours are used for projecting future needs. Nonclass laboratories are a graduate facility; therefore, graduate student credit hours are used for projecting future needs. Finally, support spaces are perhaps a facility common to graduate and undergraduate students; therefore, weighted student credit hours are used.

Classroom space projections utilize the projection of classroom contact hours generated by the whole student population. The method for projecting building requirements in classrooms is outlined below with an example:

$$\text{Utilization ratio} = \frac{\text{Existing classroom space}}{\text{1967-68 total classroom contact hours}}$$
$$= \frac{87,300}{58,500} = 1.49$$

$$\text{1980-81 requirements} = \text{1980-81 total classroom contact hours} \times \text{utilization ratio}$$
$$= 74,200 \times 1.49 = 110,600 \text{ square feet}$$

With this method future building requirements are established. The net floor area needed for academic facilities for future years is shown below. *(See Tables 13 and 14.)* These areas are, of course, total floor areas and encompass existing academic facilities, including those facilities that will be removed by 1980-81 or 1989.

The total net floor area lost by each academic discipline through removal of the few deteriorating academic-facilities structures — West Hall, Mason House, Psychology Laboratory, Peoples Avenue Complex, Winslow Building, and Blaw-Knox I and II — is shown below. *(See Table 15.)* If the areas lost by the removal of the deteriorating structures are subtracted from the existing academic-facilities inventory, the result is the total remaining net floor area of the academic facilities after the programed demolitions. *(See Table 16.)*

To convert the projected total building requirements into additional requirements for construction, the remaining total net floor area (after the removals) must be subtracted from the projected total building requirements. *(See Tables 17 and 18.)* These additional requirements need some corrections, as mentioned at the beginning of the discussion on establishing building requirements.

The first correction involves three academic disciplines: Humanities, Social Sciences, and Management. The projection of needs for these three disciplines is on the low side, because it is based on the existing space allocation, which is unsatisfactory. A 30 per cent increase in the total floor area of these three disciplines was decided upon. The increases will be made in class-laboratory space, which, in the case of these three disciplines, will mean classrooms with special equipment for their particular requirements.

In the case of Engineering, the projected needs of nonclass-laboratory space are on the high side, because the projections were based on an already high accumulation of space (Linear Accelerator Building, Nuclear Engineering and Science Building, Material Research Building, and so on) that need not be

TABLE 13

1980-81 Total Net Floor Area per Major Academic Discipline in Offices, Class and Nonclass Laboratories, and Support Spaces
(In Square Feet)

Discipline	Offices	Class Laboratories	Nonclass Laboratories	Support Spaces	Total
Architecture	7,000	20,000	5,200		32,200
Engineering	43,000	63,000	120,000	1,700	227,700
Humanities	12,000	500		1,400	13,900
Management	10,000		800		10,800
Mathematics	10,000		4,800	1,100	15,900
Physical and life sciences	41,000	50,000	108,000	6,400	205,400
Social sciences	6,000	3,100	700		9,800
Total	129,000	136,600	239,500	10,600	515,700
General-assignment space (*classrooms*)[a]					110,600
Total					626,300

[a] Based on classroom contact hours.

TABLE 14

1989 and After Total Net Floor Area per Major Academic Discipline in Offices, Class and Nonclass Laboratories, and Support Spaces
(In Square Feet)

Discipline	Offices	Class Laboratories	Nonclass Laboratories	Support Spaces	Total
Architecture	8,000	21,000	6,800		35,800
Engineering	52,000	67,000	156,000	2,000	277,000
Humanities	15,000	600		1,600	17,200
Management	12,000		900		12,900
Mathematics	12,000		6,200	1,300	19,500
Physical and life sciences	47,000	52,500	140,000	7,400	246,900
Social sciences	7,000	3,300	900		11,200
Total	153,000	144,400	310,800	12,300	620,500
General-assignment space (*classrooms*)[a]					121,000
Total					741,500

[a] Based on classroom contact hours.

TABLE 15

Eliminated Total Net Floor Area per Major Academic Discipline in Offices, Class and Nonclass Laboratories, and Support Spaces [a]
(In Square Feet)

Discipline	Offices	Class Laboratories	Nonclass Laboratories	Support Spaces	Total
Architecture					
Engineering	400		2,500		2,900
Humanities	6,200	300			6,500
Management					
Mathematics					
Physical and					
life sciences	7,500	7,600	25,000	3,100	43,200
Social sciences	2,500	2,200	200		4,900
Total	16,600	10,100	27,700	3,100	57,500
General-assignment space (*classrooms*)					22,200
Total					79,700

[a] Removed buildings are West Hall, Mason House, Psychology Laboratory (9th St.), Peoples Avenue Complex, Winslow Building, and Blaw-Knox I and II.

TABLE 16

Remaining Total Net Floor Area per Major Academic Discipline in Offices, Class and Nonclass Laboratories, and Support Spaces
(In Square Feet)

Discipline	Offices	Class Laboratories	Nonclass Laboratories	Support Spaces	Total
Architecture	6,100	21,000	1,500		28,600
Engineering	32,800[a]	59,400	76,100[a]	1,300	169,600[a]
Humanities	600[a]	0[a]		700	1,300[a]
Management	5,700		400		6,100
Mathematics	8,200		3,200	900	12,300
Physical and					
life sciences	25,900[a]	36,800[a]	47,600[a]	2,200[a]	112,500[a]
Social sciences	1,200[a]	0[a]	0[a]		1,200[a]
Total	80,500	117,200	128,800	5,100	331,600
General-assignment space (*classrooms*)					65,100
Total					396,700

[a] Areas affected by removal.

TABLE 17

**1980-81 Additional Requirements for Construction —
Total Net Floor Area per Major Academic Discipline in Offices,
Class and Nonclass Laboratories, and Support Spaces
(In Square Feet)**

Discipline	Offices	Class Laboratories	Nonclass Laboratories	Support Spaces	Total
Architecture					
Engineering	10,200	3,600	43,900	400	58,100
Humanities	11,400	500		700	12,600
Management	4,300		400		4,700
Mathematics	1,800		1,600	200	3,600
Physical and					
life sciences	15,100	13,200	60,400	4,200	92,900
Social sciences	4,800	3,100	700		8,600
Total	47,600	20,400	107,000	5,500	180,500
General-assignment space (*classrooms*)					45,500
Total					226,000

TABLE 18

**1989 and After Additional Requirements for Construction —
Total Net Floor Area per Major Academic Discipline in Offices, Class and
Nonclass Laboratories, and Support Spaces
(In Square Feet)**

Discipline	Offices	Class Laboratories	Nonclass Laboratories	Support Spaces	Total
Architecture	1,900		5,300		7,200
Engineering	19,200	7,600	79,900	700	107,400
Humanities	14,000	600		900	15,900
Management	6,300		500		6,800
Mathematics	3,800		3,000	400	7,200
Physical and					
life sciences	21,100	15,700	92,400	5,200	134,400
Social sciences	5,800	3,300			9,100
Total	72,500	27,200	181,100	7,200	288,000
General-assignment space (*classrooms*)					55,900
Total					343,900

44

duplicated in the future. For this reason, the nonclass-laboratory requirements of Engineering should be reduced by 50 per cent. The nonclass-laboratory space of Physical and Life Sciences may appear a little high also, but, since there will undoubtedly be an emphasis on the environmental studies and life sciences at R.P.I. in the future, the requirement will not be corrected.

The maximum growth of the School of Architecture has recently been reached. The 1989 projected requirements indicate that the School needs 1,900 square feet of office space and 5,300 square feet of nonclass-laboratory space. Since these needs are minimal in terms of formulating a master plan and since there is a planned renovation of the department's building, it is assumed that a better reapportionment of space will cover future needs. The needs of the discipline of Mathematics should be eliminated from the corrected building requirements. Computer facilities already exist in the structure that houses this department. Office-space requirements are considered minimal and will be provided for in adjacent new buildings.

The proposed master plan will take into consideration the maximum requirements — i.e., 1989 additional requirements — for construction, in order to allocate sites of an adequate size for the proposed building units. For this reason, the corrections mentioned will be made in this program. (*See Table 19.*) During the development of the actual construction programs of the buildings of the different disciplines, consideration should be given to phased construction rather than to building the whole unit at once. For this reason, both the 1980-81 and 1989 requirements are shown in this document.

TABLE 19

1989 Corrected Additional Building Requirements for Construction of Academic Facilities — Total Net Floor Area per Major Academic Discipline in Offices, Class and Nonclass Laboratories, and Support Spaces
(In Square Feet)

Discipline	Offices	Class Laboratories	Nonclass Laboratories	Support Spaces	Total
Architecture					
Engineering	19,200	7,600	40,000	700	67,500
Humanities	14,400	5,400		900	20,700
Management	6,300	2,000	500		8,800
Mathematics					
Physical and life sciences	21,100	15,700	92,400	5,200	134,400
Social sciences	5,800	6,000			11,800
Total	66,800	36,700	132,900	6,800	243,200
General-assignment space (*classrooms*)					55,900
University Library					80,000
Total					379,100

The detailed requirements for the new University Library will depend on a decision by the University on the type of library needed on the R.P.I. campus. The consultants' position with regard to future libraries is as follows. Until 1990 at least, books will remain an irreplaceable medium of information; the bulk of library business will continue to be with books. The surge of students to university libraries for concentrated disciplined study, especially at times of academic pressure, is not likely to be rendered less by technology and will probably increase.

The more technology facilitates access to information, the more will information and libraries be used. In planning the University Library building today, one should begin with the library as the institution we know it to be. Any deviation in the future should be made from this firm base. To be sure, technology will modify library buildings. These changes will involve trading of space, which dictates flexibility and demands additional, rather than less, space, which, in turn, dictates planning for expansion. The consultants, therefore, suggest a library of about 70,000-80,000 square feet of net floor area located on a site permitting expansion. This figure is based on a total enrollment of 7,000 students and takes into consideration the high number of graduate students at R.P.I. It allows about ten square feet of net floor area per student. This area is not out of line with other libraries of somewhat similar institutions. A list of libraries is outlined for comparison below. (*See Table 20.*) Note that the floor-area figures listed reflect total floor space.

TABLE 20

Data on Libraries of Institutions Similar to R.P.I.

School	Student Population	Seating	Total Square Feet [a]
California Institute of Technology	1,500	250	50,000
Carnegie Institute of Technology	4,000	1,100	100,000
Georgia Institute of Technology	10,000		223,000
Illinois Institute of Technology	2,800	486	96,000

[a] Net floor area is approximately 30 per cent to 40 per cent less than total floor area.

STUDENT HOUSING

The student-housing facilities will increase in proportion to the growth of the student population. This implies that R.P.I. will provide enough facilities to house approximately the same percentage of the student population that it houses today. Presently, the single-student population is about 4,300, and the married-student group numbers around 500. The total capacity of single-student-housing facilities is 1,722, whereas that of married-student facilities, i.e., apartment units, is 226. These numbers indicate that R.P.I. presently houses about 40 per cent of its student population. In projections of building requirements for the proposed master plan, the distinction between men and women students is not important. This distinction is necessary, however, in the formulation of individual building programs for the building units.

The assumption has been made that Troy's revitalization will favorably affect the housing market around the R.P.I. campus. This means that private developers will construct adequate numbers of apartments on the periphery of R.P.I.; nevertheless, there will be a constant need for a low-rent, minimal type of facility, particularly for single students. The reason for this is that low-rent off-campus rooms and houses will become progressively fewer due to the urban-renewal programs in the city.

Although it has been assumed that student-housing facilities will increase in proportion to the growth of the student population, a correction is suggested with regard to single-student housing in order to meet the above-mentioned need — namely, a 10 per cent increase for the already assumed expansion of the number of single students to be housed on the 1989 campus.

The forecasted distribution of single to married students comprising the student population at R.P.I. for the years 1980 and 1989 is given below. (*See Table 21.*) If approximately the same trend is assumed in the distribution of single to married students by the year 1989, R.P.I. will provide housing facilities for approximately 50 per cent of its single students and 40 per cent of its married-student population, which means housing for 2,675 and 660 single and married students, respectively.

TABLE 21

Forecasted Distribution of Single to Married Students for Years 1980 and 1989

	Single		Married		Total	
Students	1980	1989	1980	1989	1980	1989
Undergraduates	3,902	4,100	361	400	4,263	4,500
Graduates	968	1,250	962	1,250	1,930	2,500
Total	4,870	5,350	1,323	1,650	6,193	7,000

About half of the privately owned student fraternities will be forced to abandon their present quarters, due to deteriorating housing conditions in the city and high taxes, and to move to new facilities. Most likely, the trend of some of these groups to move to University-owned and -leased land and buildings will continue. This will mean further facilities for approximately 600 more single students and an increase in the total 1989 required capacity of single-student-housing facilities to 3,275.

The total capacity of existing single-student-housing facilities is 1,722. If the 300 units that are now under construction and will shortly be in service are added to this number, the present capacity will be 2,022. There are no planned removals of single-student-housing facilities, with the exception of the Quadrangle dormitories, to be removed in the far future should a decision be reached for improving the Sage Avenue and Fifteenth Street intersection. In that case, all or part of the site of the Quadrangle dormitories may be needed for road improvements. The removal of the Quadrangle will decrease the total capacity of single-student housing to 1,722. This brings the total single-student-housing additional requirements to 1,553, which is the result of the subtraction of the 1,722 remaining single-student facilities (after removals) from the 3,275 total single-student-housing requirements for the year 1989.

With regard to housing for married students, the removal of the Rensselaerwyck apartments will leave the 53 units of Bryckwyck as the only married-student housing on the campus. Therefore, the additional requirements for the year 1989 will be 607 apartment units, which results from subtracting the 53 units from the 660 required in 1989.

Of the recently constructed housing facilities on the R.P.I. campus, Burdett Residence Halls for single students and Bryckwyck apartments for married students both contain facilities that may be used to provide standards for projecting future building requirements for student housing. The total net floor area required for construction of single- and married-student housing in 1989 is computed below. (*See Table 22.*)

TABLE 22

1989 Additional Requirements for Construction of Student Housing
Total Net Floor Area for Single and Married Students
(In Square Feet)

Single-student housing	1,553 units × 225 square feet per unit = 349,325 square feet
Married-student housing	607 units × 640 square feet per unit = 388,480 square feet

CENTRAL FACILITIES

Basically, the central facilities are composed of functions that are, in a sense, both extracurricular student functions and service facilities. It is difficult in the absence of trends and patterns to project the needs of a campus for some of these functions, particularly when a new function is being introduced. This is the case with the first of the buildings considered in this category, the Performing Arts Center. In the case of the Infirmary, the old one is considered inadequate; therefore, a new structure must be planned. The administration activities are presently scattered throughout the campus; therefore, a new structure is suggested that will house all these activities under one roof. Finally, a new boiler house will be needed to provide services for the expanding campus; its size will naturally depend upon the requirements of each new building that will compose the future campus. A brief description of each of these new buildings is given below.

The actual requirements of the Performing Arts Center are not based on the growth of the student population, because it does not exist presently as a function on the campus. The unit is based on the exciting idea of bringing together the arts and technologies as a new academic undertaking. It is sponsored by the University, and a study about its form, requirements, and so on, is presently under way on the campus. For the purposes of the proposed master plan, similar experimental theater structures on other campuses have been studied, and it is assumed that a total net floor area of 80,000 square feet will be adequate.

The new Infirmary is intended to serve the needs of single students, both men and women, who are living either on or off the campus. It will contain only limited emergency facilities because of the proximity of the campus to Samaritan Hospital. It will serve as a convalescent center for those who do not require hospitalization but cannot recover properly in their quarters. This type of facility is usually sized by assuming a ratio of five beds to 1,000 students and 300 square feet of net floor area per bed, suggesting a total net floor area of 10,500 square feet ($5 \times \frac{7000}{1000} \times 300$).

The required building floor area of the Administration Building is based on a rough standard in accordance with the size of the student population that it is to serve. The area standard is stated in order to provide a location and a site in the master plan and it assumes that all administration activities will be under one roof. The student population size indicates that five square feet of net floor area per student may be adequate for all the administration facilities at R.P.I. This suggests a total net floor area of 35,000 square feet.

The Boiler House facility will be complementary to an existing one that provides services to the existing campus. For the purpose of allocating a centrally located and easily accessible site for this function, it is assumed that a total net floor area of 10,000 square feet will be needed.

ATHLETIC AND PLAYFIELD FACILITIES

Athletic and outdoor recreational activities at R.P.I. can be divided into four basic categories: intercollegiate activities, intramural activities, recreational activities (casual, informal), and required physical-education activities. All these programs use the existing indoor and outdoor facilities of the campus that were mentioned in Chapter 1. These facilities are, of course, inadequate to meet the expanding needs of the University.

R.P.I. has two indoor facilities, the Field House and the Gymnasium. The former is adequate for ice hockey; however, because of the length of the hockey season and other commitments, such as the performing-arts programs also held in this building, its use for other sports is limited. The Gymnasium is not only usually overcrowded, because of its limited size, but also unsafe in some instances.

R.P.I. requires certain indoor facilities in order to participate successfully in a modest intercollegiate sports program. Needless to say, these facilities must satisfy official regulations concerning size, illumination, and so on. They include a basketball court with adequate seating capacity for spectators, a six- to eight-lane swimming pool with adequate seating capacity for spectators, a track course (perhaps a part of the structure housing the basketball court), handball and squash courts, and wrestling rings. The structure that will house the basketball court should also be designed to accommodate indoors, during early spring, training for outdoor intercollegiate sports. All the above-mentioned facilities will, of course, need adequate shower and locker spaces adjacent to their locations.

The Athletics Department of R.P.I. has, in recent years, lost some of its fields to construction; perhaps, in the future, it may lose a few more. Therefore, a brief account of the necessary outdoor fields is given below, showing the types of facilities that should be included in the University's future construction program. The outdoor facilities for intercollegiate R.P.I. programs requiring fields of an appropriate size and furnished with a flood-lighting system are a new football field with adequate seating for spectators and a new baseball field with an adequate seating capacity. These facilities should also have rooms for changing located nearby. Football and baseball fields are usually placed near the indoor facilities mentioned above, and the football and baseball teams may both use the same changing rooms. The participation of different R.P.I. student groups in intramural sports programs may be an indicator of the popularity of certain sports and may serve as a guide for planning indoor and outdoor facilities, in addition to those for the intercollegiate program mentioned previously.

The sports that scheduled at least 100 intramural contests during the year 1967-68 are basketball, hockey, volleyball, touch-football, and soccer. Additional facilities are necessary for scheduling these contests and the practice sessions of the student groups. Some of the fields will also be used as practice fields for the varsity teams of the intercollegiate program. These fields must be concentrated in areas where central shower and locker rooms are readily available.

Another group of sports that scheduled over fifty intramural contests during the year 1967-68, are tennis, handball, and softball. Many more fields are needed for these sports and they should perhaps be located even next to the dormitories, because they are sports of an informal and casual nature and thus may be enjoyed by students at all times and during spare moments.

The last category of athletic and recreational activities at R.P.I. is the required physical-education program, with its increasing demands for facilities. This program will use all of the facilities mentioned above for the intercollegiate and intramural programs, thus making the need for these facilities even more pronounced.

There are two courses of action available to the University with regard to the basic indoor athletic facilities, i.e., a structure to house the basketball court, swimming pool, locker rooms, and so on. One is based on the possible acquisition of the New York State Armory, and the other on the nonavailability of this property.

With regard to the first alternative, it is assumed that the New York State Armory — a large structure with a column-free floor, approximate dimensions of 180 feet × 200 feet, and a possible floor to ceiling height of about 20-35 feet — may be acquired by R.P.I. This structure is situated in a strategic location between the freshman housing and the western part of the campus. After renovation, it may serve as a men's gymnasium; a more detailed study of this structure will reveal whether it can also house, in its basement or in an adjacent area, facilities such as a swimming pool, locker rooms, and the like. In this case, the existing Gymnasium will serve as a women's gymnasium.

If the New York State Armory property is not available to R.P.I., another structure will be needed. Its proper location, given the available land and the present concentration of athletic fields and other campus uses, is that area immediately adjacent to the northern end of the Field House.

NETWORKS AND PARKING

The circulatory system of the University serves two distinct elements: the pedestrian and the vehicular. These elements require a system that will make them independent of each other, unify the campus, and provide a way for the pedestrians within it to circulate unhampered by vehicular traffic. This system must recognize primary and secondary pedestrian connections between the components of the campus. These connections will direct pedestrians in easily recognizable, pleasant, unobstructed channels. Some of the primary pedestrian walks may possibly be covered, since the winters are rigorous and produce abundant precipitation; these will facilitate the free flow of large numbers of students at peak hours.

Although each university has its own particular character, the problems caused by the automobile are common to all. Students and faculty are appalled at the conversion of green areas into parking spaces but, nevertheless, expect to be able to park without cost close to their offices or classrooms. Moreover, university neighbors are disturbed by the cars associated with the university that line the front of their homes. The already critical parking situation at the campus will become even worse as the staff and student population increase.

The problems stemming from the automobile will oblige future university campuses to be separated into two categories: universities relying on a rapid-transit system for transport and those with an auto-oriented campus. Because of its size and other factors, the city of Troy will not in the near future be able to supply a rapid-transit system adequate to serve the needs of the University. Therefore, the future R.P.I. campus will be auto-oriented.

The consultants do not advocate the elimination of the automobile, an accepted institution in the life of the American university student; but, nonetheless, they do not consider logical the development of the auto-oriented campus as a conglomeration of a few buildings swimming in a sea of asphalt, like some large suburban shopping center. They advocate, rather, a campus layout that minimizes walking distances, thus reducing student movement by car.

In accordance with the growing number of students doing postgraduate work and, partly, the large number of married students, the master plan should provide parking spaces for 40 per cent of the total population of the campus (assuming 7,000 students and 3,000 staff). (*See Table 23.*) An effort will be made to provide an adequately large number of parking spaces as close as possible to the western part of the campus, where the nucleus of the academic plant is located. For planning purposes, about 300 square feet of surface area is allotted for the parking of each car (10′ × 20′ space for the parked car plus 100 square feet for maneuvering lanes, and the like).

TABLE 23

Total Projected Requirements for Parking Facilities

Year	Parking Spaces	Acres
1980	3,200	22.0
1989	4,000	27.5

Chapter 4 Physical Planning

This chapter outlines the logical sequence of thought that led to the proposed master plan. In most cases, the influence on the planning by the propositions stated in Chapters 2 and 3 (on assumptions and building requirements for the master plan, respectively) is implied; however, the relationship of Chapter 3 to Chapter 4 (building requirements to physical planning) is direct. Chapter 3 provides the sizes of all buildings used in the synthesis of the master plan.

CITY OF TROY

Troy's urban-renewal projects are particularly interesting because two of them are almost adjacent to the western boundary of the campus. Another factor of interest is the alignment of the north-south arterial highway, on account of its immediate effect on the accessability of the University.

Urban Renewal Project A, which includes an area directly west of the R.P.I. campus, has completed the stage of removing the pockets of decaying commercial, industrial, and residential areas. The project is presently in the phase of construction. Urban Renewal Projects B and C lie respectively northwest and west of the campus. The deteriorating areas have been identified, and both projects have now reached the final phase of planning requisite corrective action. (*See Map 4.*)

The New York State Highway Department has completed plans for the construction of the first portion of the north-south arterial highway from Menands Bridge, crossing the Hudson River in south Troy, to Ferry Street. The alignment of the north-south arterial highway passes by the western boundary of the R.P.I. campus, with two interchanges, one north of R.P.I. at Hoosick Street and one south at Ferry Street. (*See Map 11.*) With the expansion of the two interchanges, this artery has limited access in the vicinity of R.P.I. A more detailed plan of the north-south arterial highway's latest alignment, which affects the access, pedestrian and vehicular, of the R.P.I. campus, appears in a subsequent plan.

PLANNING PRINCIPLES

The major principles that guided the layout were concerned, first, with the existing physical conditions; second, with the possibility for expansion and flexibility for future use; and, third, with the separation of pedestrian and vehicular traffic. Particular attention was given to the large number of existing structures that were also incorporated into the over-all synthesis of the campus. In some areas, it was necessary to define exterior spaces by placing new buildings at strategic locations. New pedestrian and vehicular roads were suggested, incorporating the existing network or portions of it wherever possible. Finally, the topography played a very important role in the synthesis of the plan.

The difficulty of anticipating future requirements arises from two factors, the ever-present possibility of increased enrollment and the impact of the present rapid technological development on a university such as R.P.I. Thus, the following changes likely to occur in the academic area were considered: addition of new schools, expansion of existing schools, changes in parts of existing schools, and the grouping together of existing schools in common grounds or spaces. The first two items deal with expansion, while the remainder are concerned with flexibility.

A motor-free, central walk area was considered, which would allow the students to walk without being disturbed by automobile traffic. This pedestrian system of walkways will primarily serve all intra-school movements. Short service roads, extended from main vehicular roads to the buildings, will channel the traffic to the perimeter, away from the pedestrian.

MAP 11
City of Troy: Proposed Thoroughfare Plan

4

40

NORTH-SOUTH ARTERIAL

40

7

7

2

40

40

2

66+40

4

R.P.I. Campus

Street Classifications	Proposed	Existing
Arterial	▬	
Major Streets	▬ ▬	▬▬
Collector Streets	▬ ▬	▬▬
Interchanges	●	
Underpass	▮▮▮▮▮	

Note : Numbers identify major highways

N

0   1000   2000   3000   4000   Meters
0 1000 2000 4000 6000 8000 10000 12000 14000 Feet

DOXIADIS ASSOCIATES INC.—WASHINGTON, DC.

AXIS OF COMPOSITION

In considering the possible axis for the development of the campus, certain details must be noted. The north-south arterial highway, in addition to the steep slopes and bad subsoil conditions of the land immediately to the east of Eighth Street, presents a considerable barrier for any future campus growth to the west of the present campus. Southwest of the present land holdings of R.P.I. lies the Congress Street ravine, with Prospect Park on the other side. To the southeast lies a middle-income residential area with no recognizable demarcation among it, the University, and Troy High School. It would not be advisable for R.P.I. to plan growth toward the south because of bad terrain and the obstacle that an already established residential area presents.

East of the present campus lie two institutions: Troy High School and the Jewish Home for the Aged. Troy High School is a rather new structure built to house about 3,000 students at considerable expense to the city; it will remain on this site for a long time. The location of the Jewish Home for the Aged is not considered critical to the growth of R.P.I. due to its situation and topography. To the north of the present campus, on the other side of Peoples Avenue, lie Samaritan Hospital, Beman Park, and a low-middle-income residential area. Any growth in this direction would present difficulties.

The academic nucleus, which was first founded in the old Quadrangle of academic buildings — Sage, Amos Eaton, Greene, and Troy — started to move in a southern and eastern direction with the construction of the Science Center and the Material Research Building. The concentration of living quarters to the east of the present academic plant, such as the freshman housing (1,170 students), the Burdett Avenue housing (220 students), and the housing for married students (230 couples), will influence the location of any future buildings of the new campus. The concentration of student housing, together with the other new student facilities in the eastern section of the campus, such as the Rensselaer Union and the Field House, exerts a pull toward them. A beachhead is needed between the eastern and western portions of the campus and, particularly, in the constriction formed between the properties of Troy High School and Samaritan Hospital. (*See Map 12.*)

BOUNDARIES

The problem lies not in the need for additional land for anticipated growth but, rather, in the fragmentation of land and the absence of clear boundaries. A series of steps, including some land acquisition, has been suggested in another presentation to the University on the importance of campus unification. For control of the most critical land area, that between Fifteenth Street and Burdett Avenue, a beachhead is suggested uniting the two major land holdings of R.P.I. The University should first turn its attention to the area south of an axis formed with Sage Avenue and Sherry Road, followed by a bid for the control of the rest of the area.

Declining neighborhoods have been observed around practically all urban universities with undeclared boundaries for their growing needs. One of the main reasons for this phenomenon is university neighbors who are afraid that some day their backyards will be adjacent to a noisy laboratory wing or, even worse, to a clamorous fraternity house. This anxiety helps to depress land values, with well-known results. It is desirable, therefore, for R.P.I. to declare its intentions with regard to the size and limits of its ultimate campus. The declared boundaries of the R.P.I. campus should be Eighth Street, Peoples Avenue, Burdett Avenue, Hoosick Street, Tibbits Avenue, College Avenue, and its eastern extension. The city should be persuaded to zone this area for institutional uses. (*See Map 13.*)

CAMPUS-CIRCULATION PLAN

The campus is divided by city traffic into three parts: the first is between Eighth and Fifteenth streets, the second between Fifteenth Street and Burdett Avenue, and the third between Burdett and Tibbits avenues. Ideally, the three sectors composing the campus area should be unified, excluding all city traffic. This is not possible, however, because the two north-south arteries that traverse University land — Fifteenth Street and Burdett Avenue — are essential to the network of the city and, therefore, cannot be eliminated.

To unify the campus and permit the unobstructed circulation of pedestrian traffic within it, pedestrian bridges over Fifteenth Street, Burdett Avenue, and West Peoples Drive will theoretically be necessary. A restricted closed-circuit vehicular network of roads with limited control points will be planned as the University road system serving all the buildings of the University, and it will also provide some reserved parking facilities. Adequate parking in cul-de-sac form will be available from the campus peripheral roads. The campus perimeter will be penetrated by driveways leading to parking areas as close as possible to on-campus destinations. (*See Map 14.*)

MAP 12
R.P.I. Campus: Axis of Influence in Composition of Site

N

DOXIADIS ASSOCIATES INC.— WASHINGTON D(

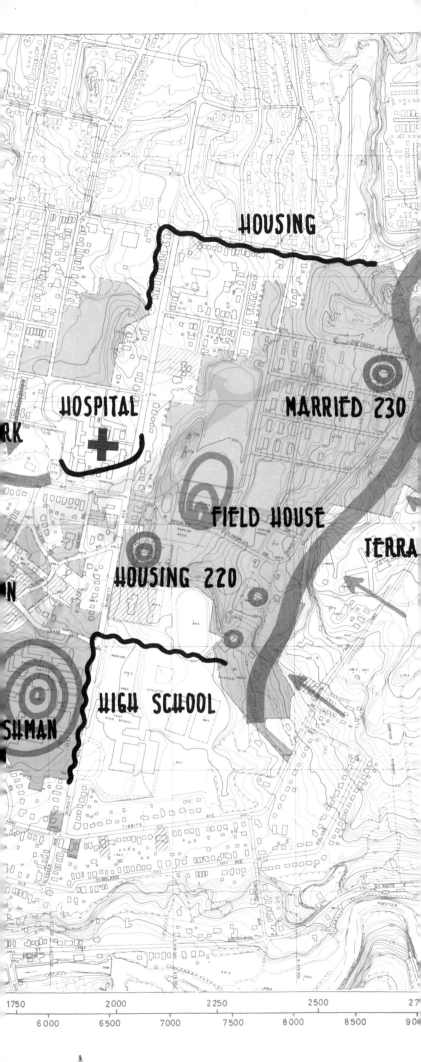

HOUSING

HOSPITAL

MARRIED 230

FIELD HOUSE

TERRA

HOUSING 220

SUMAN

HIGH SCHOOL

1750   2000   2250   2500   27

6 000   6 500   7 000   7 500   8 000   8 500   9 0

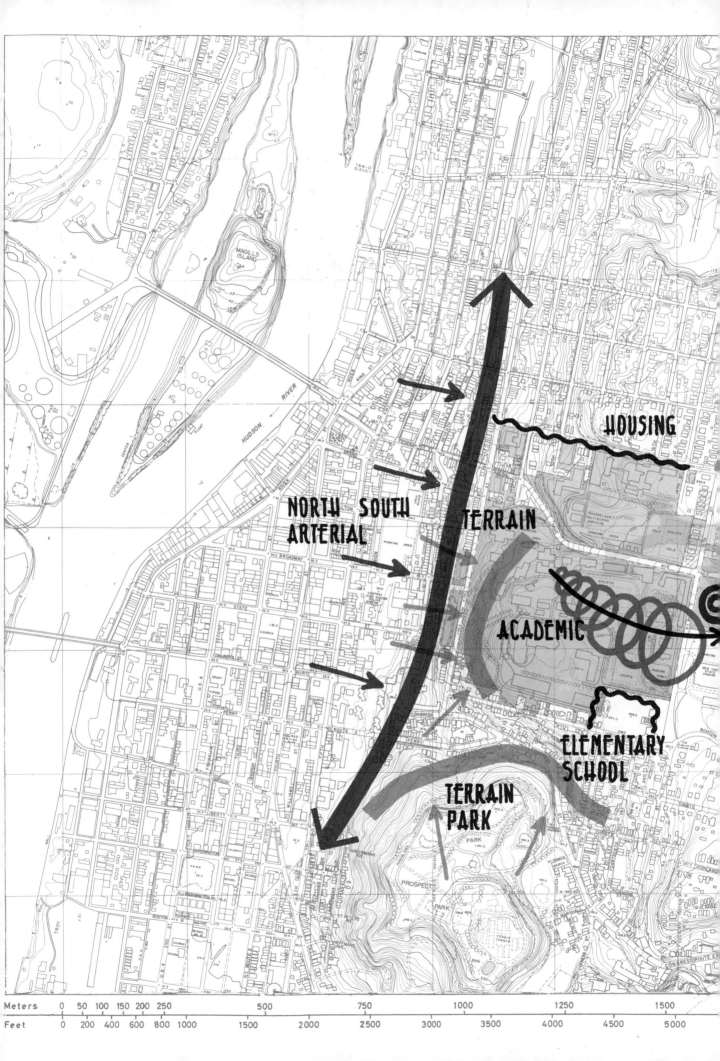

HOUSING

NORTH SOUTH
ARTERIAL

TERRAIN

ACADEMIC

ELEMENTARY
SCHOOL

TERRAIN
PARK

MAP 13
R.P.I. Campus: Proposed Unification of Boundaries

University Property

Student Fraternity Property

Religious, Related to R.P.I.

Proposed Boundaries

Suggested Improvements

N

50   2500

7500   8000

DOXIADIS ASSOCIATES INC. — WASHINGTON DC.

MAP 14
R.P.I. Campus: Basic Concept of Proposed Circulation Plan

Extension of City System

University-Service
Restricted System

Predominant
Pedestrian Traffic

Student Parking

Restricted Parking &
Building-Service Parking

Pedestrian Bridge

N

DOXIADIS ASSOCIATES INC.— WASHINGTON DC.

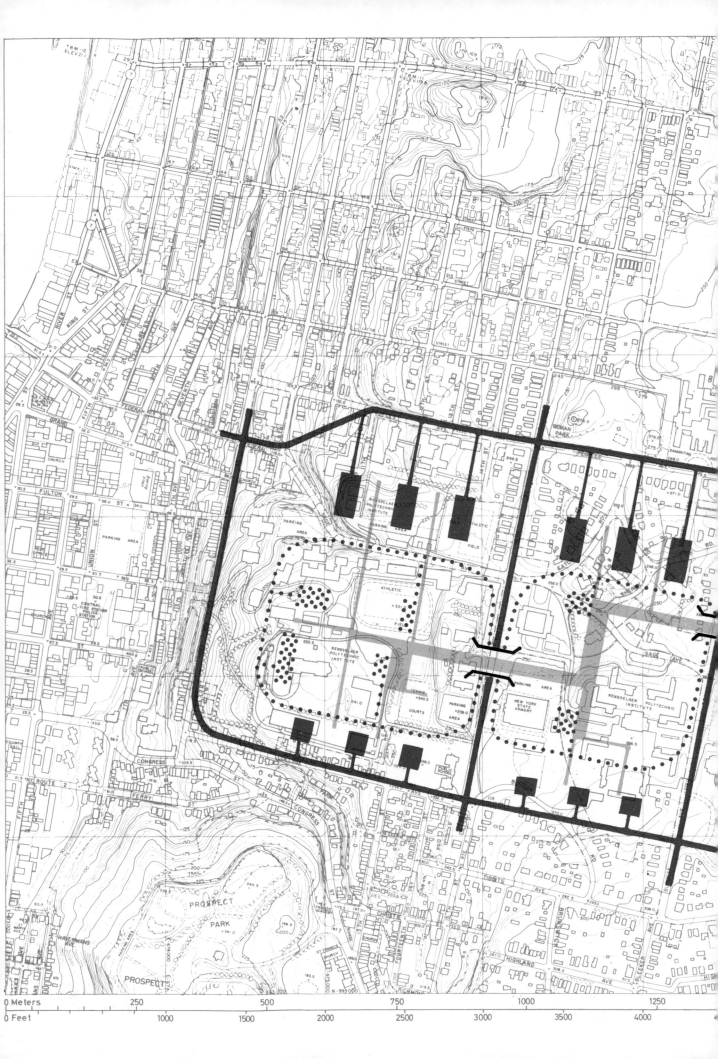

TRAFFIC IMPROVEMENTS IN CAMPUS VICINITY

Considering the basic concept underlying the city's thoroughfare plan and with the intent of improving the proposal in the vicinity of the R.P.I. campus, the consultants advised several measures that should be taken. (*See Map 15.*) First, Fifteenth Street should be the main vehicular entry to R.P.I.; therefore, direct connection of Fifteenth Street with the north-south arterial highway is needed. Two ways of connecting the highway with Fifteenth Street are possible: a northern connection — from the Hoosick Street interchange to Fifteenth Street — or a southern connection — a traffic elevation with two ramps from the Congress-Ferry Street interchange to be connected to Fifteenth Street.

Second, a proposal contained in the city's 1965 master plan suggested a bypass from Federal Street to Peoples Avenue. R.P.I. should pursue its implementation. Third, rounding the corner of Eighth Street and College Avenue is proposed in order to ease the existing steep grades at this intersection. Fourth, College Avenue should be extended toward the east. This measure would divide the proposed institutional land uses from the existing residential area and provide a clear southern campus boundary.

LAND USE

Once a land-use plan is established clearly defining the boundaries of each land-use zone, it is enforced by locating new buildings within the character of each zone. Where existing buildings are already located in the newly designed zones and where these buildings are of a different character than the one assigned, the adoption of the land-use map implies neither the demolition of the buildings found in a zone of different character nor their immediate change of use. It means only that the buildings that are out of character will not be perpetuated. Plans should be developed either for the eventual conversion of these buildings into the uses that are designated by the zones or for their virtual removal.

The already-indicated axis of growth and the restricting conditions such as topography and neighboring land uses dictate the following development of the campus. A whole system of new campus buildings and roads will be developed in a northeasterly direction, where most of the readily available land is to be found. The two most important land uses, academic and housing, should be adjacent and parallel in their growth in order that the distances between dormitories and places of instruction do not oblige the student to use an automobile. The new student and service facilities should be developed in a central location. The area that the University wisely selected for the first of the buildings in this group, the Rensselaer Union, is correct, and it is easily approached from all parts of the new campus.

The land immediately adjacent to Eighth Street, the bluff with the wonderful view of the Hudson Valley, and a strip of land immediately north of College Avenue should be designated as green buffer zones. The steep slopes of this land and the poor subsoil conditions, which make the cost of foundations prohibitive, dictate this assignment. It is possible, however, to have within these zones automobile parking platforms at different levels.

The area south of the New York State Armory should be designated as an area for outdoor physical education and playgrounds, which are badly needed in this area, near a student-housing concentration. The athletic fields and playgrounds should continue to develop in the area between Burdett Avenue, the Field House, and the zone assigned for married-student housing.

The land immediately west of Tibbits Avenue should be assigned to special projects. Functions that are not necessarily part of the academic area of the campus, but where it is desirable that they be close by, may be located in this area. These functions are generally those that create nuisance problems, such as health hazards or other risks, vibration, or noise. These are research-oriented activities and require a location at some distance from the academic and residential areas. At present, two such activities are located in this area, the Linear Accelerator Building and the Nuclear Engineering and Science Building.

Concluding, one must mention that the zones indicated in a land-use map denote the predominant assignments of land. (*See Map 16.*) A detailed land-use map, which is outside the scope of this report, is usually accompanied by a description of building heights, ratio of open land to covered area, and so on. As an illustration, one might suggest that the land assigned to student housing include a large area devoted to different types of open land, such as green areas formally planted, promenades, playfields, and student parking.

MAP 15
R.P.I. Campus: Surrounding Traffic-
Plan Proposals

| University Property | |

University Property

Student Fraternity
Property

Religious, Related to
R.P.I.

Limited–Access Highway

Major Streets

Collector Streets

Underpass or Bypass

Additional University–
Proposed Improvements

Source: Revised Master Plan, 1965,
        City of Troy, New York

N

3000

9 500   10 000

DOXIADIS ASSOCIATES INC.— WASHINGTON DC.

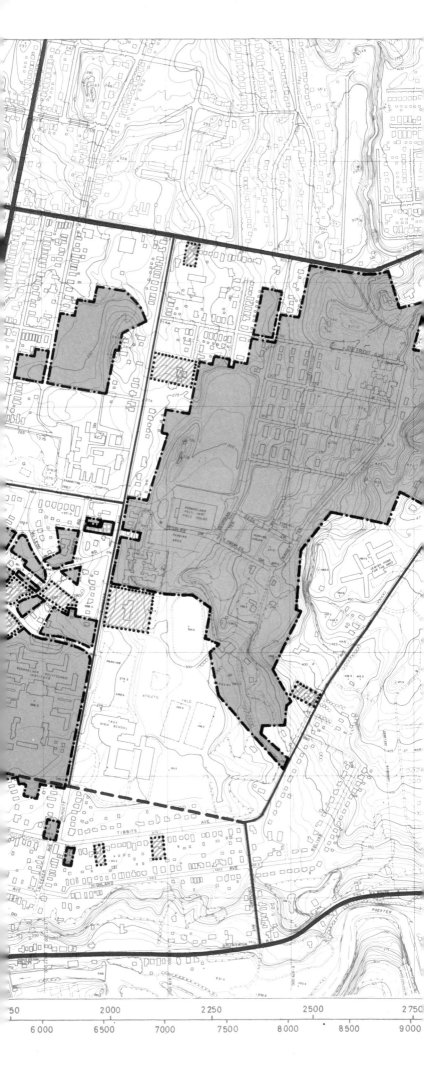

MAP 16
R.P.I. Campus: Proposed Predominant Land Uses

Academic

Future Academic

Student & Service Facilities

Student Housing

Future Student Housing

Athletic & Playfields

Future Athletic & Playfields

Parks

Special Projects Area

N

DOXIADIS ASSOCIATES INC.— WASHINGTON DC.

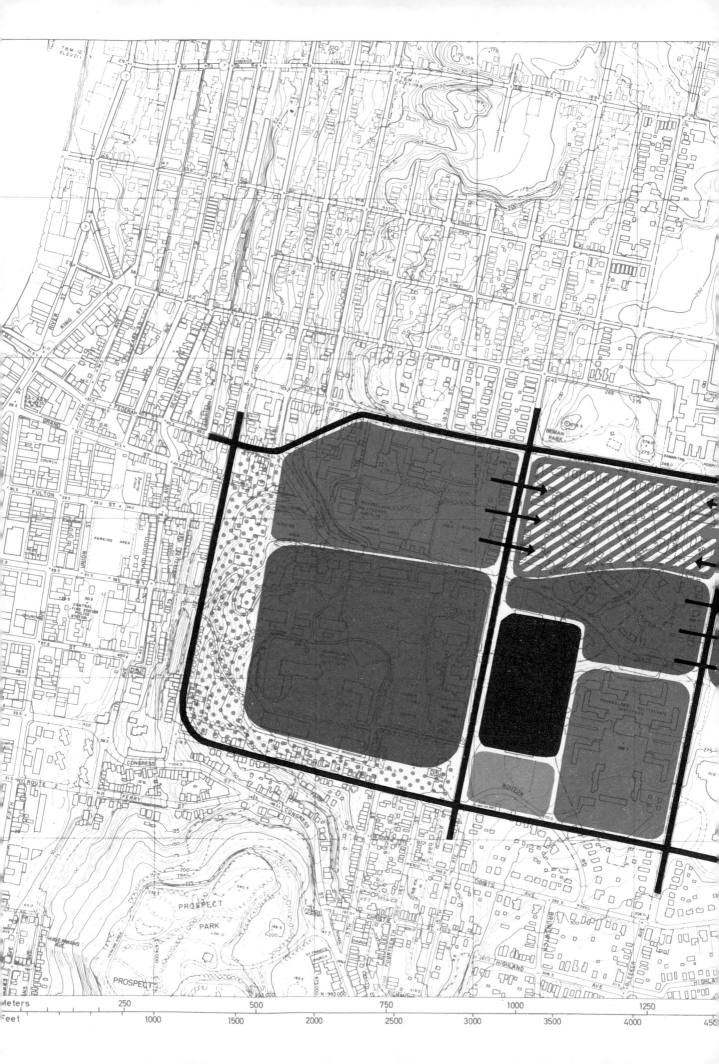

Part III

THE MASTER PLAN AND ITS PERSPECTIVE

Chapter 5 Proposed Master Plan and Program

Several alternative campus layouts were drawn with the current planning procedure, considering the axis of growth, circulation concept plan, land uses, etc. In evaluating these layouts, a mathematical model was devised based on the minimization of student movement. The model provided a complementary aid for the selection of a final solution among various reasonable alternatives, not superseding the empirical approach and the application of other meaningful criteria. One of the model's assumptions is that traveled distances can be taken as one indicator for the required length and capacity of the network system of the campus and for the costs involved in its construction and maintenance.

Two of the better-rated alternatives were presented to the University, together with a brief explanation of the model, in a study preceding this report. *(See Appendix.)* The proposal presented in this document is one of the two best-rated alternatives, with minor modifications made in order to comply with other considerations and suggestions by the University.

GENERAL SYNTHESIS

The proposed master plan is basically an elongated complex of academic buildings stretching in an east-west direction, with a parallel zone of student-housing buildings. *(See Map 17.)* It subdivides the campus into major zones dictated mainly by existing buildings or new buildings whose location was decided by the University before the consultants became involved.

The area between College and Sage avenues and Eighth and Fifteenth streets is presently used for academic activities. The existing Engineering buildings are located in the northwest section of this area. These form a binding situation for the new Engineering complex. For this reason, the new Engineering building (No. 6) is placed adjacent to this engineering nucleus. The new Engineering building's location and form complement and define the long sweep of open space that starts from the old Quadrangle eastward to the bluff adjacent to Fifteenth Street. This arrangement of the new Engineering building, two interconnected volumes with a narrow wing, allows the construction to be made in two phases, each in itself a finished building unit.

South of the concentration of existing and proposed Engineering buildings are presently located the buildings forming the University's commitment of this area to the Physical and Life Sciences. These are the Science Center and the Material Research Building. The site adjacent to the east of the Material Research Building has been committed by R.P.I. to a new Chemistry Research Building and, next to it, an office tower containing all the Science Faculty and administrative offices. The new Physical and Life Sciences complex (Nos. 8 and 9), together with the eastern part of the Chapel (Library), form the Physical and Life Sciences Quadrangle. The Chapel, which is presently used as a University Library, although not actually connected to the Physical and Life Sciences complex, will, as architectural volumes, in fact, complement each other. After the Library has been moved into new quarters, the Chapel structure will be used as a nondenominational campus Chapel.

To maintain the present campus character of open spaces, the two new academic-building complexes (Nos. 5 and 7) — i.e., one housing the new facilities for the Humanities and Social Sciences and the other the School of Management — are located on the other side of Fifteenth Street, the East Campus. The campus growth in this direction was noted earlier, when pulling forces and possible directions of growth were examined. These two functions, as the most recent schools on the campus, have the least connection with the West Campus.

Between the West Campus and the East Campus there is a group of central uses and auxiliary buildings that serve as the connecting link between the two campuses and can also be said to be the center of the cultural and social life of the campus. Most of the buildings comprising this group will be situated at a level 15-20 feet above Fifteenth Street. The buildings will consist of the existing Rensselaer Union, the new Administration Building (No. 14), the new Performing Arts Center (No. 11), the Gymnasium — the converted New York State Armory — (No. 10), and the Library (No. 4). West of the Library, under the bluff, the Modern Classroom Building (No. 3), is located closely related to the Library and to the Engineering and Physical and Life Sciences Quadrangle. The first five buildings are united with the extension of a platform over Fifteenth Street.

With regard to the Performing Arts Center, the consultants have suggested the commitment of a location near the center of the cultural and social life of the campus, since they have assumed that one of the primary purposes of this function is to provide cultural enrichment to the whole community.* To achieve this, ample exposure of this activity is needed. Therefore, it has to be located near the other poles of student attraction, such as the Rensselaer Union and the University Library, while the general public may want to come to this building often and conveniently, meaning ample parking and easy access.

A supporting factor for this location may be that this building could be administered by the Rensselaer Union itself, whose present facilities would then complement the operation of this activity. After development of the program of the Performing Arts Center and if the purpose of this function is defined to be strictly an experimental activity, with minimal student participation and an occasional performance for the community, the location to be reserved for it may be the area between the Field House and the Burdett Residence Halls.

South of the New York State Armory is located the additional boiler unit (No. 16) needed for supplying steam to the new buildings on the campus. This location is based on the availability of the New York State Armory property. If this property should not be available to the University, then an alternate location would be the area on which the first two new campus buildings, the Modern Classroom Building and the University Library, are located. When these first two new structures are built, a combined space in their basements may be provided for the new boiler unit needed for the expanding campus.

With a platform over Fifteenth Street as a pivotal point, the new and old academic- and central-facilities buildings are united with a series of walks, colonnades, alleys, and arcades at various levels following the slope of the ground. Stairs or ramps connect the different levels. In the design of this network, special care was taken to provide the walker with a variety of impressions by interweaving closed, semiclosed, and open spaces, by diversifying shapes, and by terminating vistas properly.

The present pedestrian and vehicular convergence at the intersection of Fifteenth Street and Sage Avenue and all the serious traffic problems of Fifteenth Street dictate a separation of east-west pedestrian traffic from the north-south vehicular one. This separation is most effective if the students walk on one level and the automobiles travel on another. Given the existing structures along Fifteenth Street (the Rensselaer Union, the Quadrangle dormitories, and the New York State Armory, which is to be converted into a Gymnasium), the general topography, the axis of growth, new patterns of pedestrian movements, and some aesthetic considerations, it was decided that this separation of traffic is most acceptable in the area that can be generally described as the rectangle formed by the Rensselaer Union, the New York State Armory, the Infirmary, and Sage Dining Hall. The area under the platform can be considered as a transportation center. This may be a bus stop of the future public transport system of the city of Troy and a taxi unloading area. Through stairs and mechanical ascending devices, people may be elevated to the center of gravity of the whole campus.

A series of single-student dormitories and University-owned fraternity houses face Peoples Avenue and its eastern extension. The length of this zone of single-student dormitories is parallel to the axis of growth of the academic part of the campus, thus reducing traveling distances between the dormitories and the academic area to a minimum. A wide sidewalk along Peoples Avenue passing in front of the dormitories will lead pedestrians toward the west over (or under) the north-south arterial highway into the downtown area. This is perhaps the only planned (by the state of New York) pedestrian access to town. Parking areas intervene between the single-student housing and the academic area. An effort was made to place a large number of parking spaces as close to the axis of growth of the academic area as possible. The parking areas will be used by students arriving at the campus by automobile and, of course, by the occupants of the dormitories.

The numbers appearing in each surface designated as a parking area in the proposed master plan indicate the car capacity of the parking lot (calculated on the area basis of *Table 23*). The total number of cars accommodated in the lots is a little over 4,000. It is also suggested that additional parking areas be provided in the basements of all the new buildings to be constructed on the campus.

The northeastern part of the campus is occupied by married-student housing. This area is developed along the hill that gradually rises to Tibbits Avenue, thus utilizing the magnificent view toward the west, the Hudson Valley. The areas between the parking lots, immediately south of the single-student dor-

* The consultants' assumptions were based partly on the analysis of the existing cultural life on the campus and partly on the memorandum issued by the Performing Arts Building Committee on October 23, 1968, as well as on a transcribed work session held at R.P.I. about the Performing Arts Center program on January 16-17, 1969.

MAP 17
**R.P.I. Campus: Final Phase of Pro-
posed Master Plan**

NEW CONSTRUCTION

ACADEMIC FACILITIES

CHEMISTRY RESEARCH BLDG.	①
SCIENCE OFFICES	②
MODERN CLASSROOM BLDG.	③
LIBRARY	④
HUMANITIES & SOCIAL SCIENCES	⑤
ENGINEERING	⑥
MANAGEMENT	⑦
PHYSICAL & LIFE SCIENCES	⑧
ANIMAL FACILITY	⑨

STUDENT FACILITIES

ARMORY (CONVERTED INTO NEW GYM.)	⑩
PERFORMING ARTS CENTER	⑪
INFIRMARY	⑫
STADIUM	⑬

SERVICE FACILITIES

ADMINISTRATION BLDG.	⑭
PARKING OR PARKING GARAGE	⑮
BOILER HOUSE	⑯
FACULTY CLUB	⑰

STUDENT HOUSING

SINGLE - STUDENT RESIDENCES	⑱
MARRIED - STUDENT RESIDENCES	⑲

EXISTING BUILDINGS

NEW BUILDING LOCATIONS & SHAPE DECIDED BY R.P.I.

NEW BUILDINGS

COURTYARDS, PATIOS, ETC.

ATHLETIC & PLAYFIELDS

OPEN SPACES

VEHICULAR TRAFFIC

PEDESTRIAN MOVEMENT

NOTE : NUMBER IN PARKING AREAS INDICATE CAR
CAPACITY OF PARKING LOT

N

2500

7500   8000

DOXIADIS ASSOCIATES INC.— WASHINGTON DC.

RENSSELAER
POLY INST
FIELD HOUSE

STADIUM

ATHLETIC   FIELD

TIBBITS   AVE

AVE

N.Y. ROUTE   2

1500   1750   2000   225

5000   5500   6000   6500   7000

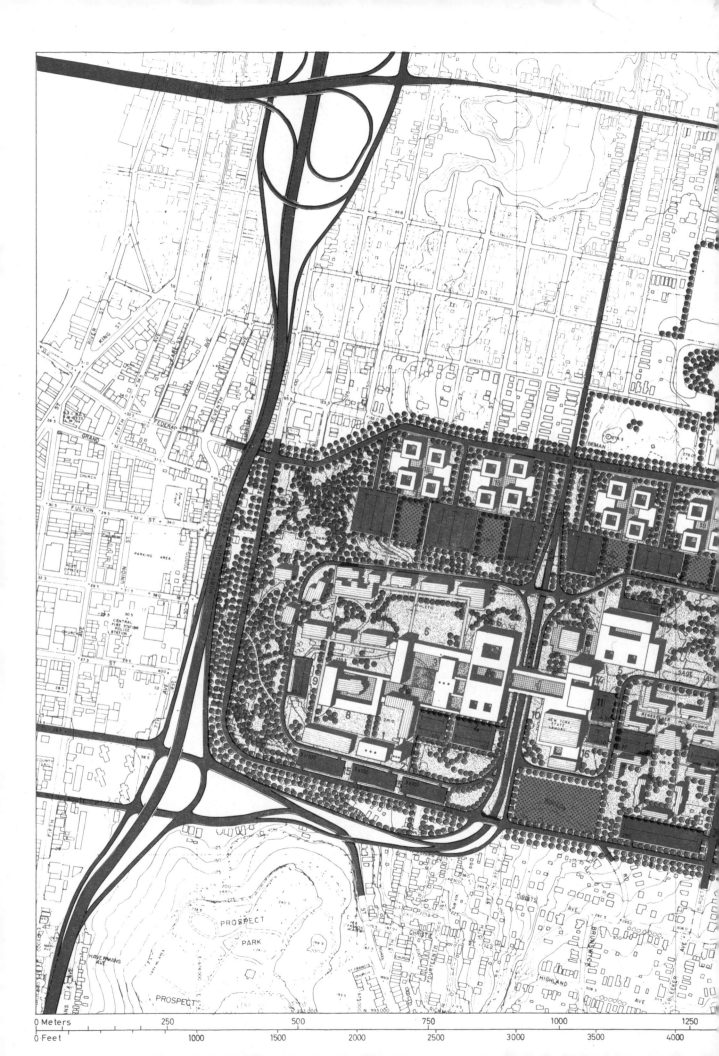

mitories, are devoted to playfields, tennis courts, softball diamonds, and so on, in close proximity for quick spontaneous use by the occupants of the nearby buildings.

The area south of the Gymnasium (the New York State Armory) is also developed for outdoor athletics. This area is adjacent to a large concentration of student housing badly in need of some areas for outdoor recreation. The main athletic and playfields areas will be concentrated north of the present Field House. The circulation system is developed along the guiding principle of separation of pedestrian from vehicular traffic. An internal vehicular road enters the main campus through two control points.

The first entrance is available if one approaches the campus from the north. In this case, after crossing Peoples Avenue and halfway to the old Fifteenth Street and Sage Avenue intersection, one may take the right ramp (the left ramp is a one-way exist only). Along the ramp is the first control point; after passing the control point, one may turn toward the west if one's destination is the old campus or toward the east, passing over Fifteenth Street, if one's destination is east and the new campus. The same principle applies to the entrance for automobiles approaching from the south, where the right lane is an entrance with the second control point and the left a one-way exit only. This internal vehicular system, which is restricted to automobiles carrying passes and to service vehicles, is a closed system permitting travel from east to west without the on-level crossing of Fifteenth Street.

With regard to this closed system, amplification is needed in connection with the parking structures along College Avenue. Because of the topography, only the roofs of the parking structures are available for parking from the internal system; otherwise, the entry to these structures is from College Avenue.

In order to complete the description of the proposed plan, a comparison can be made of the present R.P.I. campus and those of other universities, shown above, with that of the new R.P.I. campus according to the proposed master plan, shown below. (*See Table 1 and 24, respectively.*) The possible implementation program of the proposed master plan is also shown below. (*See Table 25.*) This illustrates the importance of all the phases through which a program must pass in order to materialize. It shows not only the execution of the construction contract, but also decision-making periods and limits for the actual planning of each building unit.

TABLE 24

Vital Statistics of Proposed Master Plan

School	Number of Students	Number of Students in Campus Housing	Acres	Number of Students per Acre	Built-Up Ratio in Academic Area	Built-UP Ratio in Student-Housing Area
New R.P.I. campus	7,000	4,000	390	18	19.5	14.5

The division of different building units is the same as throughout this document, i.e., academic, student housing, central facilities, athletic and playfields, and so on. The programed period commences in 1968 and continues up to the year 1990. The order of the construction priorities was determined by the University in collaboration with the consultants.

Some decision-making is required well in advance of the planning and construction period; such is the case, for example, with the pedestrian bridge over Fifteenth Street proposed in the master plan. Since the level of this bridge will affect the surrounding new buildings, it is important that this should be decided at an early stage. In some cases, the grouping of building units is required so as to enlarge the size of the construction contract. Letting out large construction contracts gives the University a considerable advantage, because this enables the participation of large, well-organized companies to compete for the contract; thus, lower quotations are obtained.

The implementation program is to be carried out in three phases. (*See Maps 18 and 19.*) The first phase for the development of the proposed master plan includes the decision-making and planning of the following building units: the Chemistry Research Building, the Modern Classroom Building, the Library, the Animal Facility, single- and married-student housing, the Performing Arts Center, and a parking garage on College Avenue.

The basic assumptions for the materialization of the initial phase are, first, that the New York State Armory will belong to R.P.I.; second, that the ground-floor levels of the Library and the Performing Arts Center will be set at the same level (approximately 255 feet) as the future footbridge over Fifteenth Street;

71

third, that the two ends of the footbridge (abutments) will be built during the first phase; fourth, that both the eastern and western ends of the footbridge will be connected by staircases with the existing level of Fifteenth Street; fifth, that the eastern portion of the footbridge (platform) will include pedestrian connections between the Gymnasium (Armory), the Performing Arts Center, the Rensselaer Union, and the freshman dormitories (a parking garage is provided under this platform); and, sixth, that the eastern portion of the platform will include a covered walkway connecting the Library with the Modern Classroom Building. This walkway continues uncovered· to the west, providing connections with the existing campus network of pedestrian walks.

The decision about the footbridge over Fifteenth Street, as was mentioned earlier, is vital. The floor levels of the Library and the Performing Arts Center depend on this footbridge. It is not implied that the implementation of the proposed master plan actually hinges on the footbridge, but, if the bridge is seen as a future possibility, it would affect the floor levels of these buildings. These buildings should, however, also work in the future without a bridge, in case this feature never materializes.

In phasing, different indications are used in the graphic presentation showing the internal road system. The purpose of this is to show the new portions of the system at each phase. The second phase of the development of the master plan includes the decision-making and planning of the following units: the Science office building, Humanities and Social Sciences (temporary quarters in Physical and Life Sciences structure), Engineering, single- and married-student housing, the Infirmary, and a parking garage. The critical decision at this phase also is to proceed with actual planning either for the whole or a portion of the pedestrian footbridge over Fifteenth Street.

DESIGN CRITERIA WITH RESPECT TO MATERIAL AND TREATMENT

All treatments within the campus should be in keeping with the present character of the University and should reflect the objectives of R.P.I. as a University centered on technology, with a stated purpose of «instructing persons who may choose to apply themselves in the application of science to the common purpose of life.» The common purpose, in this instance, is the application of technology to the creation of a total human environment.

Treatments, in general, should be aimed not so much at enhancing the individual buildings as at producing a total meaningful environment for all the activities that might take place within the campus. In other words, the architects' fantasies, when designing the individual buildings, should be subordinated to the objective of producing a more unified, over-all result.

The aim of architectural expression should be to provide a uniform structural module applying to the buildings throughout the campus. This module should be physically expressed both in the interior and the exterior of the buildings as a unified element. The siting and arrangement of the buildings should aim not so much at emphasizing their individuality and their own virtues, but, rather, at creating visually pleasing and functionally useful spaces between the buildings.

There should be a succession of visual experiences for anyone walking along the open areas between the buildings. To the extent that this is possible and consistent with the requirements of the buildings, interior courts should be provided, with one side always open at ground level for cleaning and removing snow. Arcades should be provided on the ground floor of all buildings, and these should be connected in order to provide a continuous system of covered pedestrian circulation. Volumes should be balanced in order to produce a unified system of masses.

Some basic materials common to all the buildings should be used in order to achieve unity of character. These materials should be concrete and brick. Landscaping should have an urban character, especially in the interior of the central core that would comprise the academic buildings of the campus. This urban character would imply a number of paved plazas and planting in a more formal arrangement, as well as other secondary elements and treatments. This character would be in contrast to a freer arrangement of landscaping around the central core, in which the atmosphere of open country could be maintained.

CONCLUSION

The proposed master plan is by no means final. It is only definite in its conception and in the basic ideas and principles that dictated the given solutions. Though it is not limited to establishing land uses and major circulation elements only, it should not be thought of as depending on plans for individual buildings that may never materialize, as shown in this layout. If it determines, in advance, the exact places and masses of the buildings, a detailed circulation system for pedestrians and vehicles, and, further, some special design features, it does this in order to develop a series of planning standards that will permit control of the basic design of the various buildings and will ensure the unity of the campus.

3d PHASE

	76	1976-77	1977-78	1978-79	1979-80	1980-81	1981-82	1982-83	1983-84	1984-85	1985-86	1986-87	1987-88	1988-89	1989-90
	○														
		IS													
	○	C	IS												
		D	P	C	C	IS									
	P	C	IS												
			D	P	C	IS									
						D	P	C	IS						
									D	P	C	IS			
	D	C	IS												
				D	C	IS									
							D	C	IS						
										D	C	IS			
				D	P	C	C	IS							
	C	IS													
	D	PC	IS		D	PC	IS		D	PC	IS		D	PC	IS
	C	IS													

DOXIADIS ASSOCIATES INC.— WASHINGTON DC.

TABLE 25
Implementation Program

Division	Building Units	Estimated Cost (in thousand 1968$)	Gross Area (in thousand square feet)	1st PHASE			2d PHASE			
				1968-69	1969-70	1970-71	1971-72	1972-73	1973-74	1974-
ACADEMIC FACILITIES	Chemistry Research Bldg.	3,300	45	DP	C	C	IS			
	Science offices	2,100	60			D	DP	C	C	IS
	Modern Classroom Bldg.	5,700	86	DP	C	C	IS			
	Library	4,600	110	D	P	C	C	IS		
	Humanities and social sciences	1,700	30/17				D	P	C	C
	Engineering	3,600	90					D	P	C
	Management	450	12						D	DP
	Physical and life sciences	6,800	170							
	Animal facility	400	11	D	PC	C	IS			
STUDENT HOUSING	Single-student residences (capacity in)									
	264	2,500	95	D	P	C	IS			
	264	2,500	95				D	P	C	IS
	264	2,500	95							D
	264	2,500	95							
	264	2,500	95							
	264	2,500	95							
	Married-student residences (capacity in)									
	100	3,300	90	DP	C	IS				
	100	3,300	90					D	C	IS
	100	3,300	90							
	100	3,300	90							
	100	3,300	90							
	100	3,300	90							
CENTRAL FACILITIES	Performing Arts Center	400	10		P	C	IS			
	Administration	1,300	45							
	Infirmary	400	13							D
	Boiler House	500	15							
	Gymnasium (Renovations)	300								
	Parking		900				D	PC	C	IS
	Pedestrian footbridge			D			P			

Note : D = Decision
P = Planning
C = Construction
IS = In Service

MAP 18
**R.P.I. Campus: First Phase of Propos-
ed Master Plan**

NEW   CONSTRUCTION

ACADEMIC   FACILITIES
CHEMISTRY   RESEARCH   BLDG.   ①
SCIENCE   OFFICES   ②
MODERN   CLASSROOM   BLDG.   ③
LIBRARY   ④
HUMANITIES & SOCIAL SCIENCES   ⑤
ENGINEERING   ⑥
MANAGEMENT   ⑦
PHYSICAL & LIFE SCIENCES   ⑧
ANIMAL   FACILITY   ⑨

STUDENT   FACILITIES
ARMORY (CONVERTED INTO NEW GYM.)   ⑩
PERFORMING   ARTS   CENTER   ⑪
INFIRMARY   ⑫

SERVICE   FACILITIES
ADMINISTRATION   BLDG.   ⑬
PARKING   OR PARKING GARAGE   ⑭
BOILER   HOUSE   ⑮

STUDENT   HOUSING
SINGLE - STUDENT   RESIDENCES   ⑯
MARRIED - STUDENT   RESIDENCES   ⑰

EXISTING BUILDINGS

NEW BUILDING LOCATIONS & SHAPE DECIDED BY R.P.I.

NEW BUILDINGS

COURTYARDS, PATIOS, ETC.

ATHLETIC & PLAYFIELDS

OPEN SPACES

EXISTING VEHICULAR ROADS & PARKING AREAS

NEW VEHICULAR ROADS & PARKING AREAS

PEDESTRIAN MOVEMENT

N

FIRST - PHASE   ASSUMPTIONS

1 NEW YORK STATE ARMORY BELONGS TO R.P.I.

2 THE GROUND-FLOOR LEVELS OF LIBRARY AND PERFORMING
   ARTS CENTER ARE SET ON SAME LEVEL (APPROXIMATELY 255 FEET)
   AS THE FUTURE FOOTBRIDGE OVER 15th STREET.

3 THE TWO ENDS OF THE FOOTBRIDGE (ABUTTMENTS) SHOULD BE
   BUILT IN THE FIRST PHASE.

4 BOTH THE EAST AND WEST ENDS OF THE FOOTBRIDGE WILL HAVE
   STAIR CONNECTIONS WITH EXISTING LEVEL OF 15th STREET.

5 THE EASTERN PORTION OF THE FOOTBRIDGE (PLATFORM) INCLUDES
   PEDESTRIAN CONNECTIONS BETWEEN GYM (ARMORY),
   PERFORMING ARTS CENTER, RENSSELAER UNION, AND FRESHMAN
   DORMITORIES PARKING GARAGE IS PROVIDED UNDER THIS PLATFORM.

6 THE WESTERN PORTION OF THE PLATFORM INCLUDES A COVERED WALKWAY THAT
   CONNECTS THE LIBRARY WITH THE MODERN CLASSROOM BUILDING.
   THIS WALKWAY CONTINUES WEST UNCOVERED PROVIDING CONNECTIONS
   WITH THE EXISTING CAMPUS NETWORK OF PEDESTRIAN WALKS.

2500

7500   5000

DOXIADIS ASSOCIATES INC.— WASHINGTON DC.

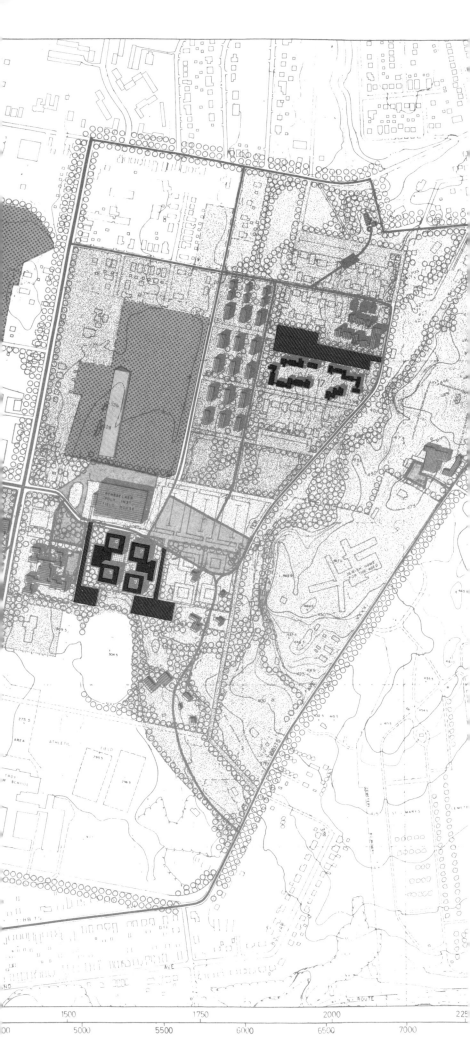

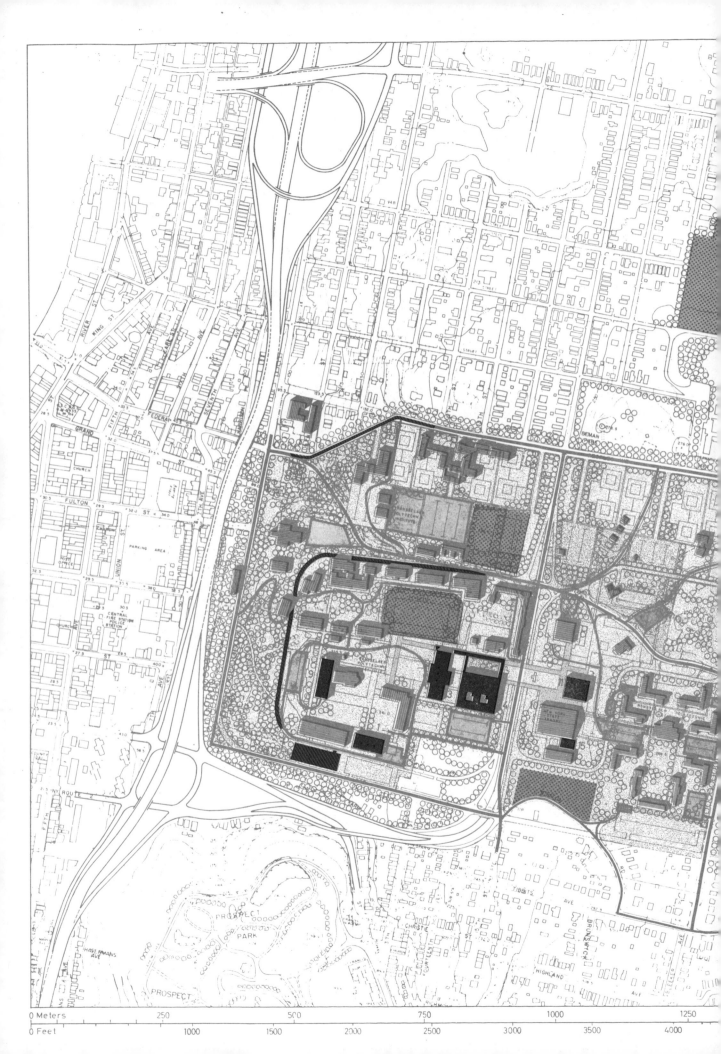

MAP 19
**R.P.I. Campus: Second Phase of Pro-
posed Master Plan**

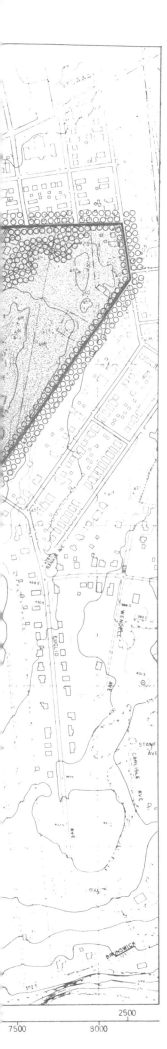

NEW CONSTRUCTION

ACADEMIC FACILITIES

CHEMISTRY RESEARCH BLDG.	①
SCIENCE OFFICES	②
MODERN CLASSROOM BLDG.	③
LIBRARY	④
HUMANITIES & SOCIAL SCIENCES (TEMP. ACCOMMODATIONS)	⑤
ENGINEERING	⑥
MANAGEMENT	⑦
PHYSICAL & LIFE SCIENCES	⑧
ANIMAL FACILITY	⑨

STUDENT FACILITIES

ARMORY (CONVERTED INTO NEW GYM.)	⑩
PERFORMING ARTS CENTER	⑪
INFIRMARY	⑫

SERVICE FACILITIES

ADMINISTRATION BLDG.	⑬
PARKING OR PARKING GARAGE	⑭
BOILER HOUSE	⑮

STUDENT HOUSING

SINGLE - STUDENT RESIDENCES	⑯
MARRIED - STUDENT RESIDENCES	⑰

EXISTING BUILDINGS

NEW BUILDINGS LOCATIONS & SHAPE DECIDED BY R.P.I.

NEW BUILDINGS LOCATIONS & SHAPE DECIDED BY R.P.I., INCLUDED IN CONSTRUCTION OF FIRST PHASE

NEW BUILDINGS

NEW BUILDINGS INCLUDED IN CONSTRUCTION OF FIRST PHASE

COURTYARDS, PATIOS, ETC.

ATHLETIC & PLAYFIELDS

OPEN SPACES

EXISTING VEHICULAR ROADS AND PARKING AREAS

NEW VEHICULAR ROADS AND PARKING AREAS

NEW VEHICULAR ROADS AND PARKING AREAS, INCLUDED IN CONSTRUCTION OF FIRST PHASE

PEDESTRIAN MOVEMENT

SECOND PHASE ASSUMPTIONS

1. A PORTION OF FOOTBRIDGE WILL BE BUILT IN THIS PHASE

N

2500

7500   3000

DOXIADIS ASSOCIATES INC. — WASHINGTON DC.

Appendix

A Mathematical Model
as an Aid to Campus Planning

GENERAL

Within the framework of the over-all study, the consultants developed and used a mathematical model as an aid to a more objective evaluation of the various layout alternatives that they had to consider before the establishment of a final plan to be proposed to R.P.I. This Appendix describes the basic concept of the model, the theoretical assumptions on which it is based, and the procedure followed when applied to the R.P.I. campus.

The model provides a complementary aid for the selection of a final solution among various reasonable alternatives. It does not supersede the empirical approach and the application of other meaningful criteria. Even within its restricted area of application, the model is bound by some limitations that call for a certain amount of caution in delineating its validity. These limitations are either inherent or incidental. The first stem from the very fact that a model is necessarily an approximate, simplified picture of what is or would be the case obtained through some theoretical generalizations and assumptions. The second are due to the more or less inevitable contingencies when applying the model to a concrete case. Such contingencies may compromise the basic information and data that go into the model and may thus diminish the relevance of the final output.

Although no model is totally exempt from the above limitations, improvement on both simulative capacity and proper application is possible and might render it a most valuable tool. With this conviction, the consultants have embarked on the elaboration of their model and its application to the R.P.I. campus. In the following pages, a succinct description of the model is provided.

METHODOLOGY

Various layouts of campus facilities are bound to generate different patterns of student traffic, even if all other factors — such as curriculum, teaching methods, and time schedule — remain constant. Each of these patterns corresponds to a sum-total of distances traveled by the students within the campus during a time unit. The basic idea from which the conception of the model originated was that this sum-total of traveled distances can be taken as a meaningful measure of the functional efficiency of each alternative campus layout, since it expresses, in a quantitative way, the coordination between the spatial distribution of the various facilities and the frequency of trips imposed among them. The lower this sum-total is, the more successful is the layout in bringing closer those facilities among which commuting is higher.

This measure is particularly meaningful if one considers that distances traveled within a campus involve not only human effort (additional energy spent by persons in motion) but also waste of time. The amount of time spent in traveling within an ordinary campus may be, and usually is, not very much, but, as it is more or less confined to the time allotted for changing classes, it may become critical to keeping the time schedule of the courses. Moreover, traveled distances can be taken as an indicator for the required length and capacity of the road system of the campus and for the costs involved in its construction and maintenance.

The effective measurement, however, of traveled distances involved in various campus layouts presents two major difficulties:

1. Travel distances cannot be considered to be homogeneous. Displacement from one facility to another usually involves both horizontal and vertical (either upward or downward) movements. These three kinds of movements differ substantially in energy and time consumption and thus·cannot be measured and added as simple spatial distances. Some movements, however, are made on foot and

81

some by mechanical means (cars, elevators, and so on). Here, again, energy and time consumption are far from being the same thing.

2. One can easily find ways of measuring, more or less accurately, the distances traveled by students within an existing campus; but the assessment of movements expected to take place within a future campus presents a more complex problem, even if the physical layout is known in advance. The increase in student enrollment, the addition of new facilities, and/or the relocation of existing ones are bound to alter substantially the pattern of movements within the campus, even if such factors as curriculum, teaching methods, and time schedule remain constant. Thus, the measurement of these movements in terms of traveled distances within alternative layouts presupposes the establishment of prospective patterns of movements most likely to occur in each alternative case.

The model devised and elaborated by the consultants for the R.P.I. campus aims especially at overcoming the above difficulties. On the basis of some reasonable assumptions, it proposes methods, first, for the conversion of various kinds of traveled distances into homogeneous quantities and, second, for the generation of plausible movement patterns in various prospective campus layouts.

A first step toward making traveled distances homogeneous was to take only pedestrian movements into account. The use of elevators is hardly ever permitted to students, at least where there are no high-rise buildings on the campus. Traveling by car represents a relatively small percentage of trips within the campus, which usually is, and should be, a pedestrian-oriented complex. Thus, all travel by car can be ignored, with the conviction that this would not affect the significance of the results too much.

The second step consisted of making all pedestrian movements commensurable, and, as already explained, these differ greatly, in terms of time and human effort spent, according to their direction (horizontal, upward, or downward). This was achieved by reducing all movements to horizontal and vertical ones and finding a proper method for measuring them on the same scale. The common measure was provided by the energy expenditure in the various types of human movement. Thus, the method of conversion finally adopted consists of multiplying vertical upward and downward distances by coefficients expressing the ratio of energy expended in unitary vertical upward and downward displacements to energy expended in a unitary horizontal displacement. These two coefficients were obtained on the basis of energy that a 154-pound person requires to perform, under normal conditions and at average speeds, horizontal, vertical upward, and vertical downward movements of equal length.

The amount of energy expended per hour for these activities is given in *Table A1*. On the basis of these values, the coefficients for the equivalence of vertical upward and vertical downward to horizontal distances have been estimated in various ways by following different assumptions. The results are shown in *Table A2*, where the assumptions in each case are also indicated. Following these assumptions, the values finally adopted for the equivalence of vertical upward and vertical downward to horizontal distances were 10.0 and 2.3, respectively.

APPLICATION OF THE MODEL ON THE R.P.I. CAMPUS

A basic input for the application of the model in campus planning consists of a set of survey data describing the characteristics of the movements of each student within the existing campus. The characteristics are function and location of the unit (classroom, lab, dormitory, office, and so on) acting as the origin of the movement, function and location of the unit acting as the destination of the movement,

TABLE A1

Amount of Energy Expended per Hour for Defined Activities
(By 154-Pound Man) [a]

Activity	Speed (in miles per hour)	Energy (in kilocalories per hour)
Standing		110
Walking downstairs	2.0	200
Horizontal walking	3.5	290
Walking upstairs	2.0	590

[a] Data from Laurence E., Morehouse and Augustus T. Miller, Jr., *Physiology of Exercise* (5th ed.; St. Louis, Mo.: C. V. Mosby Co., 1967).

Coefficients for Equivalence of Vertical Upward and Vertical Downward to Horizontal Distances

Assumptions	Vertical Upward to Horizontal	Vertical Downward to Horizontal
Assuming a 2:1 ratio for the staircase length to vertical length and including the basic metabolic energy	7.2	2.4
Same as above but subtracting the basic metabolic energy, taken as the energy for standing	9.4	1.8
Assuming 10 and 8 seconds to climb up and go down 11 feet on the staircase of the Doxiadis Associates premises	9.6	2.6
Based on work done to lift a 154-pound weight by 11 feet and assuming an efficiency of 25 per cent for the human machine	12.6	

type of locomotion during the horizontal leg of the movement (walking or by car), and school and year of study with which the student performing the movement is associated. To obtain these characteristics in the case of the R.P.I. campus, a survey was designed and implemented, by using questionnaires to be filled in by the students. They were asked to record sequentially their movements for one week within the campus by noting, in the appropriate movement sheets, the building code and room number of the origin and destination of each movement. One additional entry indicated whether the horizontal displacement involved in the movement was performed by car.

On the continuing hypothesis that no major changes would occur in the curriculum, teaching methods, and time schedule presently in use, it seemed reasonable to generate the movements within alternative future layouts on the basis of the movements taking place within the existing system. The method adopted is based on three assumptions:

1. The total number of movements in any alternative is directly proportionate to the total number of movements on the existing campus, the proportional factor being the ratio between the anticipated and the actual student enrollment. In point of fact, several proportional factors can be used, one for each faculty's enrollment.

2. The flow of student movements among the various facilities in each alternative campus layout maintains the same pattern as does the flow in the existing system.

3. The total number of trips from one type of facility to another (from dormitories to classrooms, for instance) is distributed among all pairs of functional units within these facilities, in proportion to their floor area, which is assumed to be an adequate measure of accommodating capacity.

On the basis of these assumptions, the evaluation and comparison of the various alternatives proceed through a series of steps:

First Step:	Estimate the per capita distance traveled by students within the existing campus in an appropriate time unit.
Second Step:	Determine the pattern of student movements within the existing campus.
Third Step:	Generate movements for the various layouts of the future development in accordance with the pattern of movements performed within the existing campus.
Fourth Step:	Estimate the per capita traveled distance corresponding to the various alternatives on the basis of the movements generated, as above.
Fifth Step:	Compare the per capita traveled distance obtained for the various alternatives.

The first step in the application of the model consists of the estimate of the per capita distance traveled in a week by students within the existing campus. The measurement in the R.P.I. case proceeded along the following lines. The whole complex of campus buildings was digitized: *by buildings*, each building being assigned x, y, and z coordinates, where z was taken to be the ground elevation of the main entrance of the building; *by floors*, each floor being assigned a z coordinate denoting its vertical distance from the main entrance level of the building.

For every ordered pair of floors i-j, the value

(1) $D_{ij} = h_{ij} + a_{1 \text{ or } 2} v_i + a_{1 \text{ or } 2} v_j$

was computed, where:

h_{ij} = the horizontal distance between floors i and j

v_i and v_j = the vertical distances between floors i and j and the main entrance level

a = the coefficient denoting the ratio of energy expended in a unitary vertical displacement to the energy expended in a unitary horizontal displacement; a is assigned one of two different values, a_1 or a_2, according to whether the vertical displacement is upward or downward

D_{ij} = the energy equivalent distance covered by a movement originating at floor i and terminating at floor j

Following these computations, two matrices were obtained giving respectively for each ordered pair of floors i and j the values D_{ij} and D'_{ij}, the latter being a special case of (1) where $h_{ij} = 0$.

(1a) $D_{ij} = a_{1 \text{ or } 2} v_i + a_{1 \text{ or } 2} v_j$

These second values D'_{ij} account for the cases where the horizontal displacement of a movement M_{ij} is performed by car. Another matrix is also obtained containing the number of trips M_{ij} for every ordered pair of floors i and j, as recorded in the retained sample of the survey data (floor-to-floor trip matrix).

Maps A1 and A2 illustrate (a) the layout of the existing campus facilities and (b) the elements of the floor-to-floor trip matrix, grouped together by buildings. The per capita energy-equivalent distance is then finally obtained as:

(2) $d = \dfrac{1}{n} \displaystyle\sum_{i=1}^{i=N} \sum_{j=1}^{i=N} (D_{ij} \text{ or } D'_{ij}) M_{ij}$

where:

N = the total number of digitized floors on the campus

i = the origin floor number

j = the destination floor number

D_{ij} and D'_{ij} = values found through (1) or $(1a)$ depending on whether the movement was performed by car or not

M_{ij} = the number of movements obtained from the floor-to-floor trip matrix

n = the total student enrollment

The second step, which deals with the pattern of student movements within the existing campus, consists of a square matrix P (pattern matrix) where each elements P_{ij} denotes the number of movements performed from an area assigned to function i to an area assigned to function j. To this effect, the functions of the various campus facilities such as classrooms, laboratories, offices, and so on, were classified into a total of thirty-one categories (dormitories and parking lots being lumped into one single-function category). Then, all movements codified in the questionnaires were tallied according to their origin and destination function.

The third step follows the assumptions made for the generation of movements. The movements M_{ij} (floor-to-floor trip matrix) originating at floor i and terminating at floor j can be computed as the sum of the trips originating in all the functional units of floor i and terminating in all the functional units of floor j. These movements, defined as elementary movements, are made proportional to:

1. The area A_{ik} of the functional unit V_{ik} (floor i, function k), whence they originate.
2. The area A_{jl} of the functional unit V_{jl} (floor j, function l), where they terminate.

Thus, we obtain:

(3) $M_{ij} = \displaystyle\sum_{k} \sum_{l} \dfrac{A_{ik}}{\sum_{i} A_{ik}} \dfrac{A_{jl}}{\sum_{j} A_{jl}} P_{kl}$

where:

P_{kl} is the number of trips originating in the areas allocated to function k and terminating in the area allocated to function l. (P_{kl} is obviously an element of the pattern matrix.)

MAP A1
R.P.I. Campus: Input — Existing
Pattern of Pedestrian Movement

ACADEMIC FACILLITIES
917 LINEAR ACCELERATOR
921 CARNEGIE BLDG.
922 PSYCHOLOGY LABORATORY
923 MANAGEMENT BLDG.
928 GREENE BLDG.
931 NORTH HALL BLDG.
932 BLAW KNOX II
933 OBSERVATORY BLDG.
937 RICKETTS BLDG.
938 SAGE BLDG.
939 SEISMOGRAPH BLDG.
940 HYPERSONIC LAB. BLDG.
943 BLAW KNOX I
944 TROY BLDG.
945 WALKER BLDG.
946 WINSLOW BLDG.
947 AMOS EATON BLDG.
951 MASON HOUSE
964 SCIENCE CENTER
965 WEST HALL BLDG.
967 MATERIAL RESEARCH BLDG.
968 ENG. SCIENCE BLDG.
969 NUCL. ENG. & SCIENCE BLDG.
970CD PEOPLES AVENUE COMPLEX C, D

STUDENT HOUSING
916 AUX. DORM
927 AUX. DORM
936 AUX. DORM
948 QUAD. DORM
948R CHURCH SIX DORM
963 FRESHMAN DORM AND DINING
971 "E" DORM
2026 RENSSELAERWYCK
2070 BURDETT RES. HALLS
2071 BRYCKWYCK

STUDENT SERVICES
925 STUDENT AFFAIRS
929 GYMNASIUM
930 15TH ST. LOUNGE
934 PITTSBURG (ADM.)
954 INFIRMARY
961 FIELD HOUSE

PARKING FACILLITIES
PEO PEOPLES AVENUE
G10 10TH ST.
G09 9TH ST.
FED FEDERAL ST.
NOR NORTH PARKING LOT
G08 8TH ST.
SOU SOUTH PARKING LOT
G15 15TH ST.
BOU BOUTON RD.
FRO FRESHMAN PARKING LOT
SHR SAGE AVE. PARKING LOT
SAG SAGE AVE.

Academic & Students Services Bldg.

Student Housing

Parking Facillities

Pattern of Pedestrian Movement

University Entry (North or South)

N

DOXIADIS ASSOCIATES INC.—WASHINGTON DC.

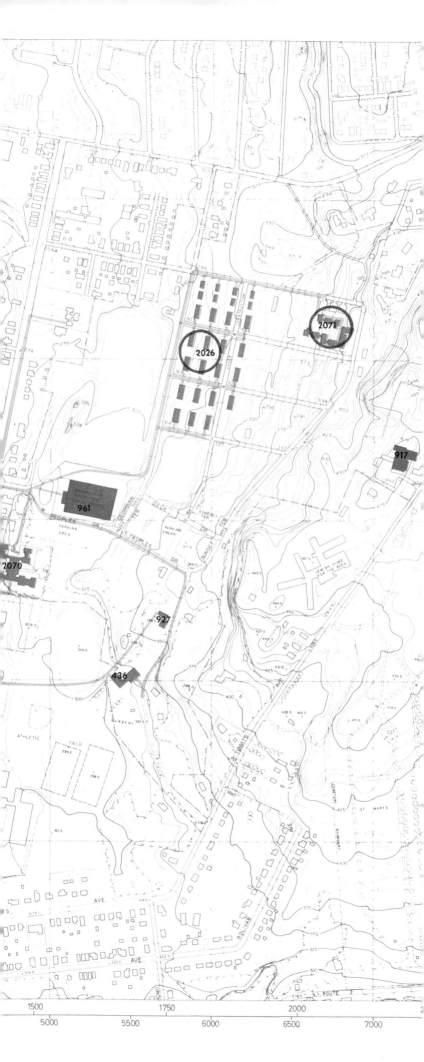

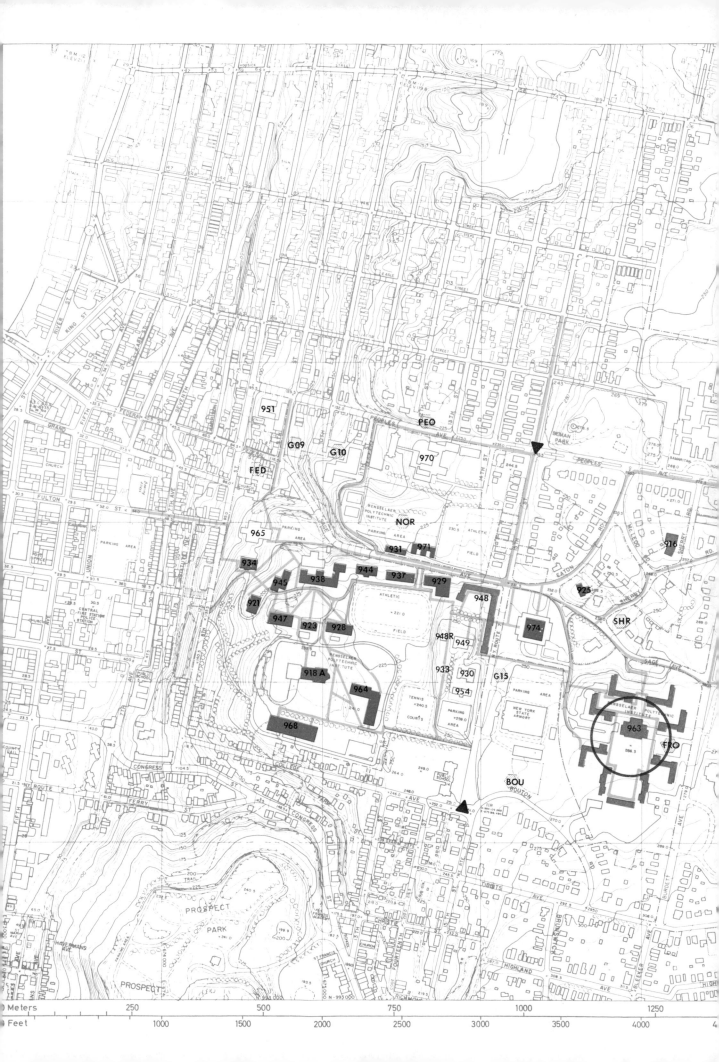

MAP A2
R.P.I. Campus: Output — Existing
Energy Expenditure Between Stations

1   GREENE, ARCHITECTURE
2   LINEAR ACCELERATOR, ENGINEERING
3   NORTH HALL, ENGINEERING
4   RICKETTS, ENGINEERING
5   SAGE, ENGINEERING
6   TROY, ENGINEERING
7   MATERIAL RESEARCH BLDG., SCIENCE
8   WEST HALL, HUMANITIES
9   MANAGEMENT
10 AMOS EATON, MATHEMATICS
11 WALKER LAB, SCIENCES
12 MASON LAB
13 SCIENCE CENTER
14 PEOPLES AVENUE COMPLEX, HUMANITIES
15 CARNEGIE, CLASSROOMS
16 LIBRARY
17 WINSLOW, ROTC
18 PITTSBURGH, ADMINISTRATION
19 STUDENT UNION
20 INFIRMARY
21 STUDENT AFFAIRS
22 15TH ST LOUNGE
23 FRESHMAN DORMITORY AND DINING
24 DORM
25 DORM
26 BURDETT AVENUE HALLS
27 DORM
28 DORM
29 DORM
30 DORM
31 MARRIED STUDENTS
32 MARRIED STUDENTS
33 GYMNASIUM
34 FIELD HOUSE
35 PARKING ON PEOPLES AVENUE
36 PARKING ON 10TH STREET
37 PARKING ON 9TH STREET
38 PARKING ON FEDERAL STREET
39 NORTH PARKING LOT
40 PARKING ON 8TH STREET
41 SOUTH PARKING LOT
42 PARKING ON 15TH STREET
43 PARKING ON BOUTON ROAD
44 FRESHMAN PARKING LOT
45 SAGE PARKING LOT
46 PARKING ON SAGE AVE.
47 NORTH APPROACH TO UNIVERSITY CAMPUS
48 SOUTH APPROACH TO UNIVERSITY CAMPUS

Graphic Presentation of Energy:
1 sq. inch = 198,400 Kilocalories

DOXIADIS ASSOCIATES INC.— WASHINGTON DC.

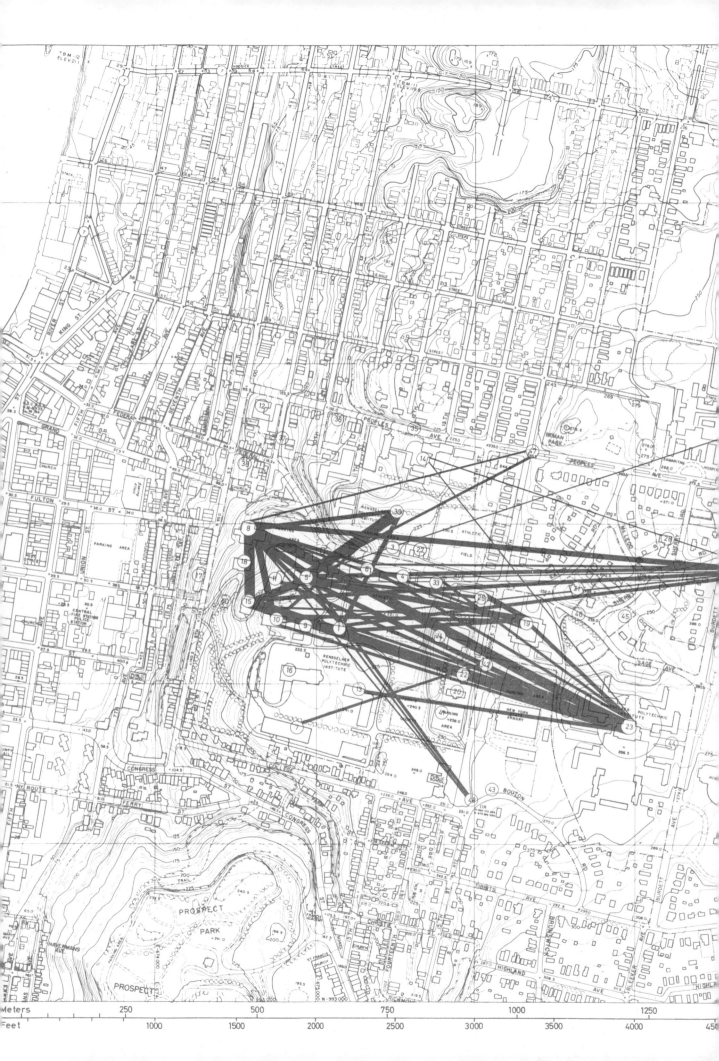

The first two summation symbols are extended to all functions k of floor i and all functions l of floor j.

$\sum_i A_{ik}$ and $\sum_j A_{jl}$ are the total areas allocated to functions k and l, respectively. Both act as

Positing $A'_{mn} = \dfrac{A_{mn}}{\sum_m A_{mn}}$, we derive:

$$(3a) \quad M_{ij} = \sum_k \sum_l A'_{ik} \; A'_{jl} \; P_{kl}$$

Formula (3a) is exemplified as follows. If floor i contains the functional areas A_1, A_2, A_3, A_4 and floor j contains the functional areas A_2, A_5, A_7, the movements originating at floor i and terminating at floor j are computed as:

$$
\begin{aligned}
M_{Ij} = \; & A'_{i1} \, A'_{j2} \, P_{12} + A'_{i1} \, A'_{j5} \, P_{15} + A'_{i1} \, A'_{j7} \, P_{17} \\
+ \; & A'_{i2} \, A'_{j2} \, P_{22} + A'_{i2} \, A'_{j5} \, P_{25} + A'_{i2} \, A'_{j7} \, P_{27} \\
+ \; & A'_{i3} \, A'_{j2} \, P_{32} + A'_{i3} \, A'_{j5} \, P_{35} + A'_{i3} \, A'_{j7} \, P_{37} \\
+ \; & A'_{i4} \, A'_{j2} \, P_{42} + A'_{i4} \, A'_{j5} \, P_{45} + A'_{i4} \, A'_{j7} \, P_{47}
\end{aligned}
$$

Floor-to-floor matrices were obtained through the application of formula (3a) for a number of layouts that had been considered as reasonable alternatives for the future development of the campus.

The fourth step closely resembles the first one insofar as the creation of the energy-equivalent distance matrices D_{ij} and D'_{ij} are concerned. The floor-to-floor trip matrix M_{ij}, as obtained through the pattern matrix in Step Three, together with the energy-equivalent distance matrices, yield for each alternative the per capita traveled distance through formula (2).

The per capita traveled distances obtained for the existing campus, as well as for the various alternative layouts of the future campus development, were tabulated and compared (Step Five). Out of the total number of considered alternatives, two were finally retained for further elaboration as giving the lesser per capita traveled distance.

Maps A3, A4, A5, and A6 illustrate these two alternatives with corresponding layouts and the elements of their floor-to-floor trip matrices grouped together by buildings. In Table A3, the results obtained for the existing layout and for the two selected alternatives are converted into three meaningful indices: distance traveled by each student in a day and the time and the energy spent in traveling by each student in a day.

TABLE A3

Results Obtained for Existing Layout and Selected Alternatives

Item	Existing Layout (4,800 Students)	Alternative I (7,000 Students)	Alternative II (7,000 Students)
Distance traveled per student per day (*in feet*)	10,700	9,320	8,880
Time spent in traveling per student per day (*in minutes*)	35	30	28
Energy spent in traveling per student per day (*in kilocalories*)	170	150	140

EVALUATION OF AN ALTERNATIVE LAYOUT

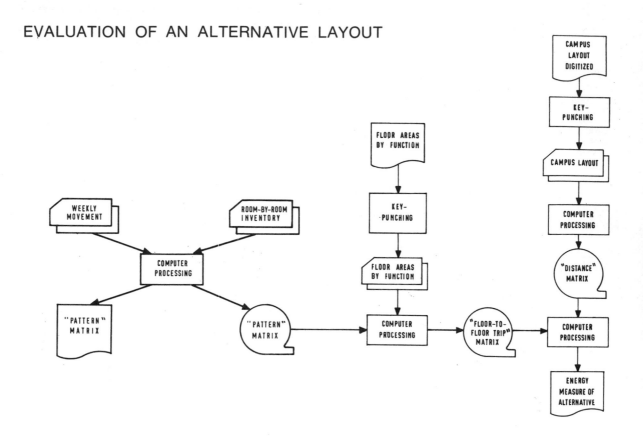

ENERGY MEASURE OF EXISTING SYSTEM

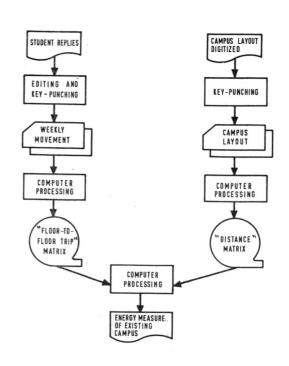

MAP A3
R.P.I. Campus: Solution «I» Input — Generated New Pattern of Movement

SOLUTION F

BUILDINGS FOR REMOVAL	
930 LO	15TH ST LOUNGE
946 WI	WINSLOW BLDG.
948 D02	WHITE SIX DORM
951 MA	MASON LAB
954 IN	INFIRMARY
965	WEST HALL
	SAGE
	SAGE DINING HALL
	OBSERVATORY

BUILDINGS TO CHANGE FUNCTION

918A LI LIBRARY, TO BE UNIVERSITY CHAPEL
929 GY GYMNASIUM TO BE GIRLS PHYSICAL-EDUCATION BUILDING
THEREFORE, WILL RETAIN ONLY 5% OF O & D MOVEMENTS
934 PI PITTSBURG BUILDING, TO HOUSE MILITARY, AIR AND
NAVAL SCIENCE
ROTC ALL O & D MOVEMENTS FROM BUILDING 946 TO BE
TRANSFERRED TO BUILDING 934
945 WA WALKER LAB, TO HOUSE ALL UNDERGRADUATE PHYS. & LIFE
SCIENCES LABORATORIES, ALL O & D MOVEMENTS TO BE
TRANSFERRED FROM BUILDING 951 TO BUILDING 945

OTHER ASSUMPTIONS

BRIDGE OVER 15TH ST ELEVATION 250

NEW CONSTRUCTION

BUILDING	FLOORS	CLASSROOMS	LIBRARY	IN-CAMPUS RESID	OFF-CAMPUS RESID	DINING & RECR	IN-CAMPUS ATHL	OUT OF CAMPUS ATHL	ROTC	MISCELLANEOUS	PARKING	OFFICES	CLASS LABS	NONCLASS LABS
		1	2	3	4	5	6	7	8	9	10	11	12	13
NA01 (ENG)	0									7				
	1											8	8	
	2											8		
NA02 (HUM)	0									10				
	1		5										10	10
	2		2									7		
	3		2									7		
NA03 (MGT)	0									4				
	1		3									5		
	2											4		
NA04 (SC OFF)	0									10				
	1											4		
	2											4		
	3											4		
	4											4		
	5											4		
	6											4		
NA05 (PH & LS)	0									10				
	1											4	2	10
	2											2	4	10
	3											2		10
NA06 (CH R)	1													8
	2													8
NA07 (CLASS)	0									10				
	1		7.5											
	2		7.5											
	3		7.5											
	4		7.5											
NA08 (GYM)						40								
NA09 (LI)	0									20				
	1		30									12		
	2		15									6		
	3		15									6		
NC10 (THE)	1					10								
NC11 (INF)	2									5				
NC12 (ADM)	0									10				
	1									5				
	2									5				
	3									5				
	4									5				
	5									5				
	6									5				
NPE1	1											60 C		
	2											60 C		
	3											60 C		
NPE2	1											50 C		
	2											50 C		
NPE3	0											50 C		
	1											100 C		
NPE4	1											100 C		
NH01	0													
	1			50 STUDENTS										
	2			50 STUDENTS										
	3			50 STUDENTS										
NH02	0													
	1			50 STUDENTS										
	2			50 STUDENTS										
	3			50 STUDENTS										
NH03	0													
	1			25 STUDENTS										
	2			25 STUDENTS										

EXISTING

 Academic & Services Bldg.

 Housing

 Parking Facilities

Pattern of Pedestrian Movements

University Entrance

NEW CONSTRUCTION

N

1	LINEAR ACCELERATOR
2	CARNEGIE
3	MANAGEMENT
4	GREENE
5	NORTH HALL
6	RICKETTS
7	SAGE
8	TROY
9	WALKER LAB.
10	AMOS EATON
11	SCIENCE CENTER
12	MATERIAL RESEARCH
13	LIBRARY
14	DORMITORY
15	ST. AFFAIRS
16	DORMITORY
17	GYM
18	PITTSBURGH
19	DORMITORY
20	DORMITORY
21	FIELD HOUSE
22	DORMITORY
23	DORMITORY
24	UNION
25	DORMITORY
26	DORMITORY
27	DORMITORY
28	PARKING ON PEOPLES AVENUE
29	PARKING ON 10TH STREET
30	PARKING ON 9TH STREET
31	PARKING ON FEDERAL STREET
32	NORTH PARKING LOT
33	PARKING ON 8TH STREET
34	SOUTH PARKING LOT
35	PARKING ON 15TH STREET
36	PARKING ON BOUTON ROAD
37	FRESHMAN PARKING
38	SAGE PARKING LOT
	PARKING ON SAGE AVE (REMOVED)
39	NORTH APPROACH TO UNIVERSITY CAMPUS
40	SOUTH APPROACH TO UNIVERSITY CAMPUS
41	PARKING GARAGE 1, COLLEGE AVE.
42	PARKING GARAGE 2, COLLEGE AVE.
43	PARKING GARAGE 3, WEST SIDE
44	PARKING EAST OR LIBRARY
45	ENGINEERING
46	HUM. & SOC. SCIENCES
47	MANAGEMENT
48	SCIENCE OFFICES
49	LIFE SCIENCES & ANIMAL FAC.
50	CHEMISTRY RESEARCH
51	MODERN CLASSROOM
52	GYMNASIUM (OLD ARMORY)
53	LIBRARY
54	SINGLE - STUDENT RESIDENCES
55	SINGLE - STUDENT RESIDENCES
56	MARRIED - STUDENT RESIDENCES
57	THEATER
58	INFIRMARY
59	ADMINISTRATION BLDG.

Graphic Presentation of Energy:

1 sq. inch = 198,400 Kilocalories

N

DOXIADIS ASSOCIATES INC.— WASHINGTON DC.

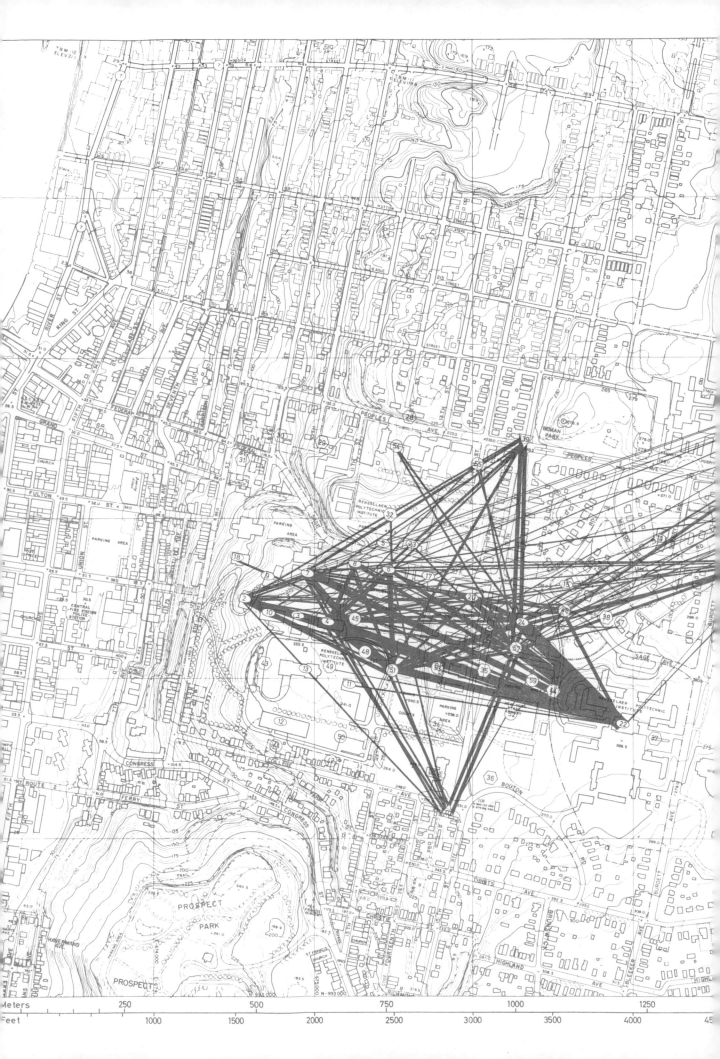

MAP A5
R.P.I. Campus: Solution «II» Input — Generated New Pattern of Movement

SOLUTION L

BUILDINGS FOR REMOVAL

938	LO	15TH ST LOUNGE
946	WI	WINSLOW BLDG.
948R	D02	WHITE SIX DORM
951	MA	MASON LAB
954	IN	INFIRMARY
965		WEST HALL
		SAGE BLDG.
		SAGE DINING HALL
		OBSERVATORY

BUILDINGS TO CHANGE FUNCTION

918A	LI	LIBRARY, TO BE UNIVERSITY CHAPEL
929	GY	GYMNASIUM TO BE GIRLS PHYSICAL-EDUCATION BUILDING; THEREFORE, WII; RETAIN ONLY 5% OF O & D MOVEMENTS
934	PI	PITTSBURG BUILDING, TO HOUSE MILITARY, AIR, AND NAVAL SCIENCE ROTC ALL O & D MOVEMENTS FROM BUILDING 946 TO BE TRANSFERRED TO BUILDING 934
945	WA	WALKER LAB, TO HOUSE ALL UNDERGRADUATE PHYS. & LIFE SCIENCES LABORATORIES, ALL O & D MOVEMENTS TO BE TRANSFERRED FROM BUILDING 951 TO BUILDING 945

OTHER ASSUMPTIONS

BRIDGE OVER 15TH ST ELEVATION 255

NEW CONSTRUCTION

BUILDING	FLOORS	CLASSROOMS 1	LIBRARY 2	IN-CAMPUS RESID 3	OFF-CAMPUS RESID 4	DINING & RECR 5	IN-CAMPUS ATHL 6	OUT OF CAMPUS 7	ROTC 8	MISCELLANEOUS 9	PARKING 10	OFFICES 11	CLASS LABS 12	NONCLASS LABS 13
NA01 (ENG)	0									7				
	1											5	3	
	2											5	3	
NA02 (HUM)	0									10				
	1	5										5	10	10
	2	1										5		
	3	1										5		
	4	1										5		
NA03 (MGT)	0									4				
	1	1										2		
	2	2										1		
	3											3		
NA04 (SC OFF)	0									10				
	1											8		
	2											8		
	3											8		
NA05 (PH & LS)	0									10				
	1											4	10	10
	2											2		10
	3											2		10
NA06 (CH R)	0													8
	1													8
	2													8
NA07 (CLASS)	0									10				
	1	10												
	2	10												
	3	10												
NA08 (GYM)	1						40							
NA09 (LI)	0									20				
	1		30									10		
	2		10									5		
	3		10									5		
	4		10									5		
NC10 (THE)	1					10								
NC11 (INF)	1									5		5		
	2									5				
NC12 (ADM)	0									10				
	1									15				
	2									5				
	3									5				
	4									5				
NPK1	1										60 C			
	2										60 C			
	3										60 C			
NPK2.	1										50 C			
	2										50 C			
	3										50 C			
NPK3	0										100 C			
	1										100 C			
NPK4	0										100 C			
NHD1	0													
	1			50 STUDENTS										
	2			50 STUDENTS										
	3			50 STUDENTS										
NHD2	0													
	1			50 STUDENTS										
	2			50 STUDENTS										
	3			50 STUDENTS										
NHD3	0													
	1			25 STUDENTS										
	2			25 STUDENTS										

EXISTING   NEW CONSTRUCTION

 Academic & Services Bldg.

 Housing

 Parking Facilities

 Pattern of Pedestrian Movements

 University Entrance

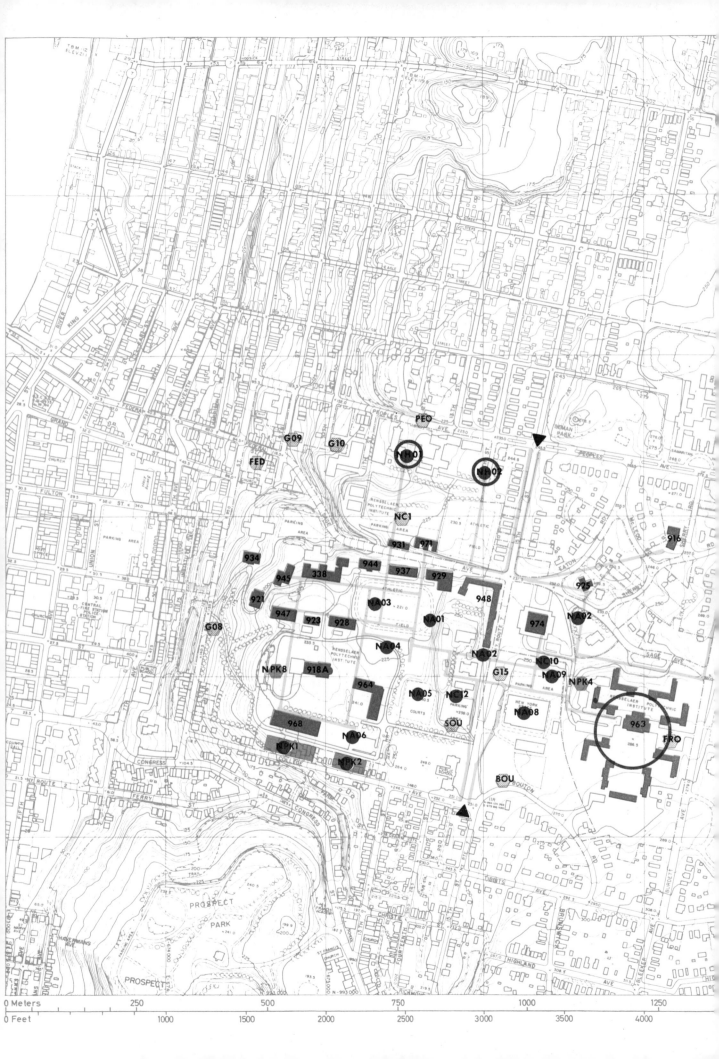

MAP A6
R.P.I. Campus: Solution «II» Output — Future Energy Expenditure Between Stations

1   LINEAR ACCELERATOR
2   CARNEGIE
3   MANAGEMENT
4   GREENE
5   NORTH HALL
6   RICKETTS
7   SAGE
8   TROY
9   WALKER LAB.
10 AMOS   EATON
11 SCIENCE   CENTER
12 MATERIAL   RESEARCH
13 LIBRARY
14 DORMITORY
15 ST. AFFAIRS
16 DORMITORY
17 GYM
18 PITTSBURGH
19 DORMITORY
20 DORMITORY
21 FIELD HOUSE
22 DORMITORY
23 DORMITORY
24 UNION
25 DORMITORY
26 DORMITORY
27 DORMITORY
28 PARKING   ON   PEOPLES AVENUE
29 PARKING   ON   10TH STREET
30 PARKING   ON   9TH STREET
31 PARKING   ON   FEDERAL STREET
32 NORTH   PARKING   LOT
33 PARKING   ON   8TH STREET
34 SOUTH   PARKING   LOT
35 PARKING   ON   15TH STREET
36 PARKING   ON   BOUTON ROAD
37 FRESHMAN   PARKING
38 SAGE PARKING LOT
    PARKING ON SAGE AVE (REMOVED)
39 NORTH   APPROACH TO   UNIVERSITY CAMPUS
40 SOUTH   APPROACH TO   UNIVERSITY CAMPUS
41 PARKING   GARAGE 1, COLLEGE AVE.
42 PARKING   GARAGE 2, COLLEGE AVE.
43 PARKING   GARAGE 3, WEST SIDE
44 PARKING   EAST OR LIBRARY
45 ENGINEERING
46 HUM. & SOC. SCIENCES
47 MANAGEMENT
48 SCIENCE   OFFICES
49 LIFE SCIENCES & ANIMAL FAC.
50 CHEMISTRY   RESEARCH
51 MODERN   CLASSROOM
52 GYMNASIUM   (OLD ARMORY)
53 LIBRARY
54 SINGLE - STUDENT RESIDENCES
55 SINGLE - STUDENT RESIDENCES
56 MARRIED - STUDENT RESIDENCES
57 THEATER
58 INFIRMARY
59 ADMINISTRATION BLDG.

Graphic Presentation of Energy:
1 sq. inch = 198,400 Kilocalories

N

DOXIADIS ASSOCIATES INC. — WASHINGTON DC.

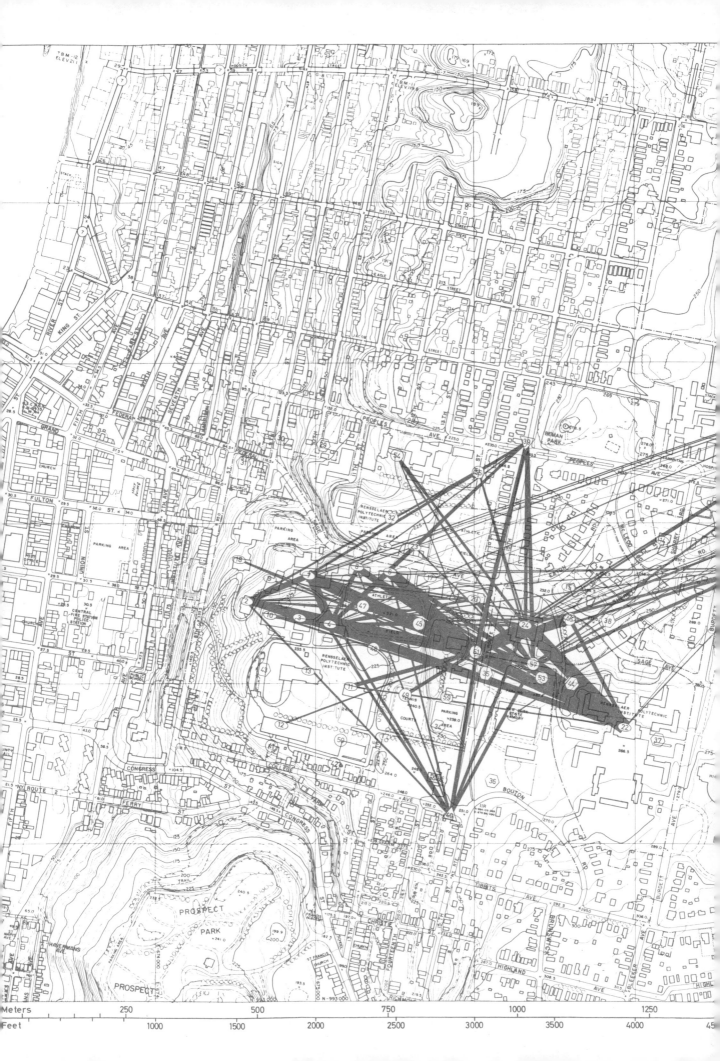

Because of the extent of the computations involved in the application of the model, all steps previously described were implemented and processed on a digital computer. The interconnection among the various inputs, outputs, and processes is summarized in the run diagrams of *Table A4*.

SOME FINAL REMARKS

The quantity and quality of the survey data are of primary importance for a reliable application of the model. It must be noted, however, that, in the case of R.P.I., the quantity of replies obtained was poor. There were only 538 replies out of a total of 4,798 students, according to the Registrar's fall, 1968, report. Furthermore, the distribution of replies in the strata (school and year of study) was very uneven, thus creating a very serious sampling problem. The quality of the replies presented a worse problem. The great majority of filled questionnaires was incomplete and called for substantial discarding.

The consultants decided to discard, at the very outset, all replies where both the building and the room code numbers were missing in some movements. Thus, of the 538 replies obtained, only 278 were retained. The replies retained were then divided into two categories: replies properly filled in (amounting to only 159) and replies where the building code number was properly filled in, but where some movements were recorded by using the floor number instead of the room number (amounting to 119). In view of the above, even though the replies in the second category were carefully edited before processing, it is felt that the results of the application of the model must be regarded and commented upon with an awareness of the dubious quality of the survey data.

Despite the limitations and drawbacks imposed by the inadequacy of the survey data, the model proved a helpful device. It confirmed the reasonableness of the considerations made with the empirical approach, on which the study was mainly based. Should more reliable data be made available, the consultants are confident that the application of the model, perhaps elaborated a bit further, might be a very useful tool for campus planning.

About the Author

Doxiadis Associates, internationally known consultants on area development and ekistics (the new science of human settlements), have been involved in the planning of such cities as Pakistan's new capital at Islamabad and the replanning of such cities as Rio de Janeiro, Detroit, and Philadelphia, as well as the Rio de la Plata basin, the Great Lakes megalopolis, and other larger areas. Other projects include those that have been associated with the International Bank for Reconstruction and Development, the United Nations, and the governments of France, Ghana, India, Spain, the Sudan, Syria, and Egypt, in addition to those of Brazil and Pakistan.